Praise for
What You Really Want, Wants You

Following the principles put forth in this book will help us all to become the universal humans we were born to be. It's a step toward the conscious evolution of our planet. I endorse this work fully.

—Barbara Marx Hubbard, president, Foundation for
Conscious Evolution, www.barbaramarxhubbard.com

Dr. Toni provides a spiritual tool to improve our lives and make the world a better place. I recommend it highly.

—Dr. Kathy Hearn, community spiritual leader, United
Centers for Spiritual Living

Dr. Toni provides a practical blueprint to getting whatever you want. This is cutting-edge thinking based on ancient spiritual truths and is a powerful guide for applying the Law of Attraction. Apply what she teaches and you will prove to yourself that what you really want, really does want you!

—Sharon Wilson, chief inspiration officer and founder,
Coaching from Spirit Institute, www.coachingfromspirit.com

Toni La Motta's What You Really Want, Wants You *is far more than a book of inspiration and motivation. It's a prayer, a deep soul prayer that can reconnect you with who you really are.*

—Judith Sherven, PhD, and Jim Sniechowski, PhD, best-selling authors of *Be Loved for Who You Really Are*, www.judithandjim.com

In the journey of the soul, the discovery of the real wealth in life is the greatest gift. Dr Toni helps you discover your self. Insights in this book are a joy to be cherished.

—Dr. Harry Morgan Moses, author, *It's So Easy When You Know How*, www.newthought.com

What You REALLY Want,
Wants You

ALSO BY DR. TONI LA MOTTA

Recognition: The Quality Way, ASQ Quality Press, (February, 1995)

DR. TONI LA MOTTA WEB SITE

www.tonilamotta.com

The Web site contains other Dr. Toni LaMotta products
as well as portions of this book
available on MP3 and CD

DR. TONI LA MOTTA BLOG

www.inlightenedenterprises.com

What You REALLY Want, Wants You

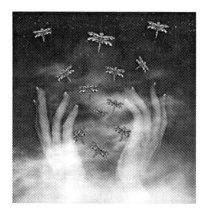

Uncovering Twelve Qualities You Already Have to
Get What You Think Is Missing

Dr. Toni LaMotta

iUniverse, Inc.
New York Lincoln Shanghai

What You REALLY Want, Wants You
Uncovering Twelve Qualities You Already Have to Get What You Think Is Missing

Copyright © 2007 by Toni LaMotta

iUniverse books may be ordered through booksellers or by contacting:

iUniverse
2021 Pine Lake Road, Suite 100
Lincoln, NE 68512
www.iuniverse.com
1-800-Authors (1-800-288-4677)

Because of the dynamic nature of the Internet, any Web addresses or links contained in this book may have changed since publication and may no longer be valid.

The views expressed in this work are solely those of the author and do not necessarily reflect the views of the publisher, and the publisher hereby disclaims any responsibility for them.

ISBN: 978-0-595-45429-7 (pbk)
ISBN: 978-0-595-70050-9 (cloth)
ISBN: 978-0-595-89742-1 (ebk)

Printed in the United States of America

Grateful acknowledgment is made to:

Lloyd Strom and Marsha Sutton (www.sacreddays.org) for *The Fear to Faith Process*, reprinted by permission.

Lisa Umberger, singer/songwriter for permission to use *Thanks and Glad Praise* from the album *Softly & Tenderly.*

Cheryl L. Costello-Forshey for permission to use her poem, "The Most Beautiful Flower."

To my students and clients, (my real teachers)
who have put these principles into practice in their lives

Contents

Acknowledgments

To Marie Picciuto, Judy Lukin, Robyn Lynn, Nancy Myers, Ingrid Russell, Andrea Page, and Jennifer Jordan—great friends and mastermind partners who have stood by me through the changes in my life, believed in me, and keep supporting me no matter what.

To the mentors who inspired me by their writings or recordings: Ernest Holmes, Eric Butterworth, Emma Curtis Hopkins, Joel Goldsmith, and Esther Hicks (Abraham).

To those whose lives made me want to make mine more meaningful, especially Sri Bhagavan and Amma, Barbara Marx Hubbard, Tony Robbins, Joe Vitale, and Dr. Michael Bernard Beckwith.

To Dr. Kathy Hearn, the original inspiration for using the twelve qualities and an avid supporter of my life process.

To Marcia Sutton, spiritual director and inspiration for truly changing my life from fear to faith, and Lloyd Strom for creating the process that has helped not only me, but the many students whom I have had the privilege to teach.

To Shirley Edwards, life coach extraordinaire, who cheered me on and supported me in believing more in myself and for reminding me that "it is enough."

To the members of my churches in Alpine, Calif., and Sarasota, Fla., and in particular to my practitioners: Gay Beauregard, Jake Dean, Charlene Crawley, Janet Hyman, Eileen Kemp, Bruce Matten, Beth Fink, Teri Endres, Gerry Greig, and Kathy Rowe, who took these principles to heart and proved their value.

To my many editors and readers: To Betsy Marx, for her eagle-eyed editing, Toni Gaeta for her continual enthusiasm over the work as well as a great gift of seeing the details that I miss. To Maria Clemente, for hours and hours of support both written and verbal. And, most of all, my sister, Connie, whose insights and questions crafted a much better book than was originally drafted.

Meaning of the Dragonfly

A number of years ago, I began to be given lots of gifts that had images of dragonflies. I'm not really sure how it all got started, but, like most things in my life, I wanted to see what meaning I might make out of this. I did some casual searching on the Internet and talked with friends who have studied the meaning of symbols in our lives. I discovered that there is much about the dragonfly that makes it inspirational.

The Power of the Dragonfly

Dragonflies spend most of their lives underwater before they take their full form and reach for the skies. Like the butterfly, the dragonfly undergoes an amazing process and has become a symbol of trans-formation. Dragonflies are unique in that they reflect colors in ways that create new and different perspectives. They teach us to look beyond what is, to see what can be, and to use that power to trans-form ourselves and reach for our dreams.

In Native American astrology, the dragonfly spirit means you must consciously make an effort to express your hopes, dreams, needs, and wishes. We would call those intentions, goals, manifestations—so, the dragonfly represents continual growth.

The dragonfly has a beautiful, jewel-like coloring, which takes time to develop. In our lives, it often takes maturity for our own true colors to come forth. Transformation then becomes an awakening of what is already within us, rather than a change to something new.

The ability to reflect and refract light and color has caused the dragonfly to be associated with magic and mysticism, manifesting life from the unknown realms in every culture.

The dragonfly's magic is the power of light and all that has ever been associated with it. Dragonflies remind us that we are light and can reflect the light in powerful ways if we choose to do so. Life is never quite the way it appears, but is always filled with light and color. Once we truly understand that we are light, we begin to reflect that in ways we never could have before imagined.

On a larger scale, the dragonfly can cause us to question the illu-sion that we call reality, particularly that part of our reality which limits our ability to grow and create transformation in our lives. We are cocreators. What we really want already exists when we recognize what is really real. The dragonfly reminds us that ordinary physical reality isn't all that is available to us. There is *always* more than we can imagine. Its rainbow wings remind us that we actually live in an ever-expanding spiritual universe.

The dragonfly reminds us to "let our light shine." It brings the brightness of inspiration and the wonder of colorful new insights. Whenever you see a dragonfly, it is my wish that you may be reminded of who you truly are and allow yourself to shine.

To hear more about what I've learned as the lesson of the dragonfly, pick up your free thirty-minute MP3 audio postcard at

http://audiopostcard-006.com/Y.asp?8682996X1166

Bookmark this site. It's worth it, I promise.

Introduction:
From Success to Significance

For years I've been pondering a dilemma that came as a result of studying both success literature and spiritual teachers. I've been on a spiritual path most of my life. I have doctorates in religious studies and divinity, and have taught world religions for years at a university. More important, I have meditated almost daily since I was thirteen, and the many books I've read and messages I've heard have verified my inner knowledge. My gift to those I have taught is my ability to synthesize information from many and varied sources, which I have shared with countless audiences over the past thirty-plus years.

Most "spiritual teachers" tell you to live in the *now* and "allow" things to happen. Almost every spiritual tradition has teachings about living in the moment and surrendering to what is.

I've also read a lot and studied with teachers of "success," who, on the other hand, emphasize how to "make" things happen: set goals, focus on them, and take action to attain them.

So I've often wondered, *Is there a contradiction here? Many people teach that you can visualize and get what you want; others say let go and let God. Which is right?*

For those who don't like setting goals, or for those who have set them and haven't been as successful as they would like in attaining them, I have good news: There isn't as much of a contradiction between living in the now and making things happen as appears at first. It all depends on our personal perspective, and mainly where we are in our spiritual journey of growth.

Over the years, I have studied many different teachings that describe the stages of spiritual development. In my early days of studying theology and mystics like Saint John of the Cross and Saint Teresa of Avila, I learned that there were the purgative, illuminative, and unitive ways. These steps of spiritual growth were defined as clearing away negative influences, opening to a life of virtue, and finally experiencing union with the divine.

Years later, I met Ron Roth, mystic, spiritual teacher, and healer, who explores these teachings in a more modern context and labels not three but five stages in his teaching: awakening, purification, illumination, dark night of the soul, and Divine Union. These parallel the steps found in the class book, *Mysticism*, by the scholar Evelyn Underhill.[1]

More recently I heard a simplified version of spiritual unfoldment from both Marsha Sutton, who was my spiritual director, and from one of my favorite teachers, (the founder of the Agape International Spiritual Center in Culver City, CA.) Dr. Michael Bernard Beckwith. Interpreting what I have learned from all of these, I now describe the stages as:

1. I'm not in control. I'm a victim. I ask, "Why me?" Things in my life keep happening *to me*.

2. I co-create my reality. I am powerful. I understand the Law of Attraction. Things happen *by me*.

3. I surrender to something higher than myself and become a vehicle for service. Things happen *through me*.

4. I recognize my oneness with all there is. Things happen *as me*.

This book can serve you regardless of where you find yourself on the journey of personal transformation. As you move in and out of these four stages, however, you may read, hear, and understand what seem to be different messages.

Therefore, let's look at each of these stages in greater detail so you can understand them and determine at which stage you are most of the time.

1. To Me

In this stage, life seems to be happening *to you*. At its extreme, you feel powerless, a victim of circumstances, and all you can see is how life failed you.

When the boss yells, the stock market falls, or the dinner burns, the question is always the same: "Why me?" You view every circumstance, every relationship, and in particular every failure through the distorted lens of the victim. Have you ever looked up at the heavens in frustration and yelled, "Why me, God?"' If so, you are familiar with this first stage. Check to see if somewhere in your life you are living from the "why me" perspective, where you are letting someone, something, some circumstance, affect your sense of well-being. You are in this stage when you believe that something outside of yourself is doing something to you. It may be a belief in a god that causes things to happen, the devil, superstition, the day you were born, the numerological chart, the cracks on the ground, your parents, or your partner.

If you are in this stage, you may find some of the messages in this book quite challenging, but I invite you to keep reading and see if you can discover a way of life that leads to greater freedom. This book will challenge how you see yourself and the world. I invite you to take this challenge.

2. By Me

Somewhere along the line you may have discovered, perhaps through pain or through insight, that you are a part of something bigger than yourself. It's a universe, and it operates orderly and lawfully. At this stage you become a manifester or a manipulator. You learn how to manipulate energy. You learn how to use the laws of the universe and, as I once heard Dr. Michael Beckwith in a lecture say, "That things don't just happen—they happen Just." This is where you learn that your thoughts and emotions create your reality. You begin to learn to "name it and claim it." You see it and you have it. You learn about visualization—seeing and feeling what you want, then watching it enter your experience. You make things happen at this stage.

But many people stop at this stage. When things aren't manifesting, it's because they've reverted to first-stage thinking. They think something outside of them, some circumstance, has to change. Or they hold onto old beliefs about themselves or old grudges.

Stage two is exciting because as you work with your visualizations and affirmations, and reprogram your old beliefs, you begin to have an awareness that the universe is good and harmonious. This awareness gradually becomes second nature. It takes time, but when it happens you begin to move into stage three, where you become a channel or instrument of the spirit.

If you've seen the movie *The Secret* or have read and studied the Law of Attraction, you'll understand this stage. In essence, the Law of Attraction states that what you think, feel, and act upon on a consistent basis becomes the experience of your life. That gives you both control over and responsibility for your life. Those who have some experience with this law will most appreciate this book. Still, even they may wonder why all their intentions and goals haven't become their reality—yet!

3. Through Me

At stage three, the good that begins to happen goes beyond your imagination, beyond what you can visualize, beyond what you can make happen. A life force, an energy, flows through you, and it is nothing short of miraculous. You begin to let go of the need to make things happen and instead "allow" them to unfold. That is part of what this book is leading you to experience.

4. As Me

And then there's stage four. This is Jesus Christ consciousness. This is Buddha consciousness. This is Gandhi consciousness. This is living in a state of union rather than a state of separation. This unity interconnects all of life, so we approach all of life with reverence and gratitude.

I'm still grappling with this stage, both in understanding it and in living it. I have glimpses. At this stage we know our oneness with all of life. This is truly a mystical stage, a sense of at-onement with the presence of God where you realize there is no difference nor is there any separation between this one life. There is only the life of God.

(If you find the *God* word challenging, look to heal whatever belief you may have; but in the meantime, just substitute the word *good* whenever you see the word *God*. Occasionally, I will use the word "Go(o)d" for emphasis.)

Though we move in and out of all four stages, we can't transcend any one of them until we have mastered the stage before. A majority of the people with whom I have done coaching and spiritual direction are moving between stages two and three, aiming to manifest greater health, wealth, and relationships, and fuller self-expression. This brings us back to the topic of setting goals.

If what you want to manifest is concrete, in the external realm of things or experiences, you can't just sit and think about what you want and feel your way into having it. You also need to take *action* to have those things unfold. But the kind of action that occurs in stage three is *inspired action*. That's different from the nose-to-the-grindstone hard work most people think they need to engage in to make something work. Inspired action is more a matter of allowing things to unfold and paying attention when something is inviting your active response, like a nudge to make a phone call, or to respond to an advertisement or invitation.

If what you want to manifest is in the internal world, such as greater serenity in life or growth toward what many call enlightenment, then according to mystical teachers, you need grace as well as action. You can learn to allow grace in your life. You can do so by acknowledging a higher power or presence and asking for the gift of grace.

I have noticed over the years that when I set goals, I often achieve what I set out to accomplish as long as I plan my work and work my plan. But I have also noticed that when I focus more on the essence of what I want (in other words, what I *really* want), my intentions and desires are answered in ways far better than I could have dreamed or imagined. If I don't try to determine exactly how the picture should look, but concentrate instead on the feeling or inner quality that I ultimately want to experience, I'm amazed that the results sometimes seem magical and certainly more significant.

If you like to set goals, then by all means do so. But if you are honest with yourself, you'll find that it's not the new car, for example, that you really want; rather, the meaning or significance of your desire is what you will experience or feel—freedom, for instance—when you have the new car. If you focus on getting a new car this year, you just may get one. But if you focus on freedom, I can guarantee that you'll get a lot more than the car. Focusing on *qualities* rather than on goals or resolutions is a powerful tool for achieving what you really want and what you really want is even more significant than what you were once calling success.

I have seen this truth, which I call a Spiritual System for Success, play out over and over again. This system teaches you to let go of the small ideas, or the *hows*, you think must happen, and the way you think life should work. What you really want is usually far bigger and more significant than what you would have defined as success. Have you ever achieved a goal you once set and then found yourself saying in effect, "Is that all there is?"

Setting specific goals can prevent you from getting the true essence of what you want. You can never truly know all that is actually possible if you limit yourself to what you *think* you want.

This book will teach you how to identify and focus on the qualities or essence—in other words, what you *really* want. My aim is to help you discover that the things you think are your current goals are only a symbol of what it is you are actually seeking. When you reach a goal, the world calls it success. When you experience greater abundance, balance, beauty, freedom, joy, love, order, peace, power, unity, wisdom, and wholeness, then you know true significance.

You'll learn how to take the steps that feel right and call to you to achieve what you want, without trying to determine "how" your dreams will come. You will learn to trust that the laws of the universe always work to give you what you focus on. You will also discover that what you think is missing is already within you, once you learn how to access it. I promise that a rewarding, significant journey awaits you.

Chapter 1

Be, Do, Have

What would your life be if it were exactly as you've always wanted it to be? Take some time to sit quietly and begin daydreaming. What would your perfect day look like? How would you be dressed? Who and what would be part of your life? Can you see yourself in every aspect of this dream-come-true scenario? What are you doing? Who is around you? How are you feeling? If you take time to do this visualization exercise, you may notice that this life is so good that it almost seems real.

Touch it, taste it, feel it, visualize it—and it's all yours! If you've read any of the success books or listened to success teachers, you've encountered that mantra before. They all seem to say that once you set goals, in order to achieve them you need to see yourself as having already obtained them. This method has worked fairly well for me and for the clients I have worked with, and we've all found that creating vision boards, treasure maps, or pictures of what we want and focusing on them each day often produces the desired results. Perhaps you have found this to be true as well.

Have you also found sometimes that though you set goals and focus on them, for some reason you don't achieve them?' For example, you set the goal of improving your physical health through losing weight and exercising more. Or, you set the goal of improving your finances; achieving the goal is always just "out there"—on its way to you, but not yet in your pocket. Or the love of your life for the moment is your cat or dog, and that's just not satisfying. Or maybe the job of your dreams is still only a dream.

Goal-setting works—for some people, some times. But it is not a 100 percent method that works all the time for everyone. So, what's missing? Some of the newer books on goal-setting reveal part of the answer. They instruct that instead of looking at what you want to *have* in life, you first have to *be* the one who can *have* what you want. But these books don't tell you how to *be* so that you can *have* your heart's desire.

The secret to achieving the life of your dreams is be, do, have. And, as you'll discover in this book, *being* is living from the inside out.

Being is not something you have to add to yourself, nor is it something you have to do in order to achieve success. Being is a matter of recognizing and uncovering what is already in you.

Being demands that you awaken to, know, and accept who you really are. It's not outside you. You won't experience being when you do or have what you think you need to do. When you realize that it's already inside you, you begin to do things differently; and then the thing(s) you want to have will more readily manifest themselves. Whatever you think you need to reach for outside yourself is already within you. Let me illustrate.

When a child feels sick or sad, and she reaches for a favorite teddy bear and starts to hug it, she begins to feel better. In fact, she begins to feel loved.

But where was the love? Certainly not in the hunk of material and buttons that was manufactured in some faraway teddy bear factory. The love the child feels was already inside her. When the child hugged the teddy bear, she became aware of that love.

Adults are just like the child hugging the teddy bear. Everything you need *is already in you.* You can have all of your dreams. You can reach all of your goals—once you find and accept the divine qualities that are innately within you. Accepting that truth is the first step you need to take to find the love for yourself in your own heart.

"Divine qualities? In me?" you may be asking. "I'm not so sure."

We' have all covered ourselves with so many false beliefs: "I can't," "It won't work," "I shouldn't"—that we no longer really know what *is* possible. It's time to wake up and uncover and discover who you *really* are. It's time to accept your magnificence.

Focus

What's your first thought upon awakening each day? Is it about possibilities or problems? What do you put your focus on?

When something happens that you didn't anticipate and probably didn't want (like a minor accident), what's your response?

Are any of the following statements familiar to you?

- "This shouldn't be happening."

- "Life is unfair."

- "When will good things come to me?"

- "Why do things like this always happen to me?"

- "I knew things were going too well. I've been waiting for the other shoe to drop."

Whew! Keep that up and guess what? You'll get more of the same! Maybe not other accidents, but more experiences to *prove* that your belief about yourself as a victim is right.

Our minds are like magnets, attracting to us the things we think about. So if we think often enough that "'bad things happen to good people,'" then things we choose to label "bad" will keep happening.

It's a law, just like gravity. It always works. There is great power in focus. *Whatever we focus on increases.*

Science supports this as well. Fundamental to contemporary quantum theory is the notion of the observer effect, that the observer influences and actually changes what is observed. Some scientists even believe that there is no phenomenon *until* it is observed. The "Copenhagen interpretation" of Quantum Theory developed by Niels Bohr, Werner Heisenberg, Wolfgang Pauli, and others says two basic things:

1. Reality is identical with the totality of observed phenomena (which means reality does not exist in the absence of observation), and

2. Quantum mechanics is a complete description of reality; no deeper understanding is possible.[1]

Oversimplified, it means that by focusing on a particle we actually bring that particle into existence. There is no need for effort or strain.

The implications of this view of the observer effect are profound, because it is asserting that before anything can manifest in the physical universe, it must first be observed. Since observation cannot occur without the preexistence of some sort of consciousness to do the observing, this interpretation of the observer effect supports the idea that the physical universe is the direct result of *consciousness*.

These quantum physicists and the teaching of ancient wisdom bring us this good news: What we think about, we bring about. Thus, it becomes clear that we need to put our attention on what we *want* instead of what we *don't want*. The truth is, *whatever we focus on increases in our lives*. Whatever we send out, then that's what we start to get back.

So if you focus on what else could go wrong in your life, the "else" will show up! If you focus on why life always gives you a bum rap, then life has no choice but to give you what you are paying attention to—that is, the very thing you don't want. If you focus on what there isn't enough of, not only will this thinking produce more of the same, but it will also leave you with an awful feeling. "I don't have enough money. There isn't enough time. My self-esteem is so low." Does this list sound familiar?

If you focus on lack, for example, you will create more of it in your life. Likewise, if you focus on abundance, you will create more of that as well. Have ever noticed that those who talk about not having enough money usually don't? To paraphrase the master teacher, Jesus, who frequently spoke of the importance of faith in order to be healed, "It is done unto you as you believe." We show outwardly what we truly believe inwardly by the words we speak. We may say we want good health, for example, but if our conversations always center on our illnesses, or our fear of illnesses, then that's what we'll bring about in our life.

It takes a little practice to listen to yourself carefully. Are you thinking, talking, and dreaming about what you don't have?

How can you change that habit? Here's the alternative. If you focus on what you are grateful for, you begin to see *more* things to be grateful for. If you focus on possibility, then you open yourself up to *more* possibility. However, if you simply believe things are possible but do not see them in the present, they will remain just that—possible—always somewhere out there, eluding you. This is the mind-set that says, "Someday my prince will come!"

Gonna come someday, but not quite here yet. "Sure, I believe it is possible to be healthy—and I'm waiting for it to happen. I believe that wealth is possible, and someday I'm going to experience it." Possibility thinking keeps you in the not-yet-having mode! This is what happens to most people who set goals. The goal is always in the unattainable tomorrow. You may have set goals and found yourself taking the actions necessary to achieve them. You've worked hard and kept your nose to the grindstone until you've achieved them. Much of the time, hard work does pay off! But sometimes you have set goals, kept your focus on them, and worked just as hard, but you never met your goals. You're left to wonder why they never came to fruition.

Keep reading. You'll begin to see the importance of focus.

Ernest Holmes, in his famous text *The Science of Mind,* says,

> Take time every day to see your life as you wish it to be, to make a mental picture of your ideal. Pass the picture over to the Law and go about your business, with a calm assurance that on the inner side of life something is taking place. There should not be

any sense of hurry or worry about this, just a calm, peaceful sense of reality.[2]

To help you focus on this mental picture, take a marker to a white board and put a big black dot in the center. What do you see there? Most people see only the black dot, because they become so focused on it, rather than seeing all the white space that has the potential to become what they cannot already see. The black dot is like the goals that we set. When we narrow our attention to what we want to achieve, we miss the infinite potential of all that may be available to us.

I'm not against goals. There is power in goal-setting. But I suggest that you stop setting them until you recognize that what you *really* want is usually far more significant than the concrete goal you are setting.

Whatever we focus on in life increases. The problem is that most of us focus on the wrong things. We spend most of our lives looking at the things we don't have and don't want, and then wonder why we have more of the same.

So, what do we need to do instead?

Take the Test

There is a "testing kit" within you to discover where your attention generally lies. You do not have to write anything. The process involves only a willingness to be honest with yourself.

Answer this question honestly: Where and to whom do you express your love? To your spouse or partner? Your children? Your boss? Your company? Your church? Your president? Your country? Yourself? Your God? If you are a loving person, then the fruit of that love is gratitude.

Ask yourself, "Is gratitude my most prevalent feeling throughout the day?" If your thoughts are truly focused on love, on Go(o)d, they will express themselves in gratitude. Gratitude will be your predominant feeling as you move throughout your day.

Now, if your predominant though unconscious thought is criticism or judgment, it will manifest itself as resentment. Ask yourself, "Are resentments my major feeling?" Whom and what do you criticize? Whom or what do you judge? Whom or what are you constantly trying to figure out? Your spouse or partner? Your boss? Your children? Your company? Your church? Your president? Your country? Yourself? Your God?

Do you criticize the trivial? Traffic, prices, the checkout line, the media, the school system? The appearance or actions of others? Do you constantly criticize yourself? Do you ever say to yourself, "How dumb could I be? How stupid I am!" Or, "Look at me, I can't even do …" and you fill in the blanks. If you are critical of others or yourself, the result of that criticism is the feeling of resentment.

So, the test is: Where is your attention generally found? Does it produce gratitude? Or does it produce resentment? Which feeling do you usually express? Are you loving, or are you critical?

If you find subtle ways in which you are more complaining than joyful, then there is no need for further analysis. This is what we as humans do to ourselves. For example, it's not wrong if you get angry at something that happens. The problem is when you get angry over getting angry and start condemning yourself. Throughout the ages, spiritual teachers have taught that one of the primary purposes in life is to grow more and more into loving ourselves and others. Jesus, the master teacher, when talking about the greatest commandments, said we were to "Love your neighbor as yourself" (Matt. 22:39), which presupposes loving ourselves.

Goal-Setting

How does this self-test relate to your goals (or if you'd rather, use the word *manifestation* or *outcome*)? Most people who set goals don't actually achieve them. As stated, in order to accomplish things in the outside world, goal-setting is important, and I notice that every success teacher explains that as their first step.

Then why are people coming in droves to ministers like me, and counselors and friends, bemoaning the fact that they don't have in life the things that they most want, the very goals that they've set?

Because when most of us set goals, we begin to focus even more acutely on the fact that there is "not enough."

Making New Year's resolutions is a good example of this. When most people make resolutions, they focus on what hasn't been working and what needs to be fixed or changed. With all the gifts of the holiday season and all the bills coming due, it is also the time of the year that many begin to focus even more acutely on "not enough." Think about what you might say to yourself each New Year's Eve. "The year is ending—what have I accomplished?" If you are like most people, your answer is likely about what you haven't' done that you wanted to do, or thought you should have done. Or you look forward and make a list that says, "This year I'm going to …," which is usually another list of the things you are berating yourself for. It's full of the things that you don't *have* enough of or things which you don't *do* enough.

How many New Year's resolutions have you been able to achieve?

I used to find this really confusing. I know all about setting goals, making them specific, writing them down, and making a definite plan for carrying them out. I've done all that. In fact, I wrote them out and read them daily. But I began to see that sometimes goal-setting and determination often brought me (and the hundreds of people I have counseled over the years) tension and emotional pain.

When I focused too much on goals, and the things I didn't have or wasn't being or doing, I started to believe that I was not okay. I thought I would be—when I got my next degree, lost excess weight, or conjured up the husband that my wish list described.

Without the proper understanding behind this exercise, goal-setting supported my *discontent* with what was and narrowed my vision of what could be.

Would you like to set goals in a way that makes a real difference in your life? Here is what you need to do and think about differently.

Goals work *if* you are able to see yourself as already having them. Visualization is a very effective tool. But here is the challenge with visualization. If what you visualize is something you see in the distant future rather than as something already present, you are setting yourself up for inner conflict.

Furthermore, feeling always manifests more strongly than the visualizations we have. Our focus is often more on the side of what's not here than on what we want. We have so many unconscious beliefs and patterns that keep us from having what, on a conscious level, we think we want. So, picturing what you don't yet possess as if you already possess it works if you don't have contradictory thoughts and feelings.

Many people think they already are focusing on what they want and thus wonder why they aren't getting it. When this happens, it's because they have subconscious thoughts that are stronger than what is conscious. The trick is to make conscious what you believe, so if it isn't serving you, you can decide to change it. That's where the abundance of spiritual tools we have available to each of us comes in handy.

You must bombard your conscious mind with the new image of what you want to experience in your life. One obstacle is that the old way of being is entrenched in your subconscious. By learning to put your attention on what you do want rather than on what you don't want, you can begin to change the entrenched pattern. It's time to realize that what you do want is just an outward representation of what you already naturally possess. You've just forgotten it or buried it. (Remember the child and the teddy bear?)

Beliefs are like magnets. They attract themselves. Your erroneous beliefs that you don't have what you want have attracted lots of experiences that "prove" you right. So when you change what you believe, you change your experience. The best way I know to change beliefs is to change what you put your attention on.

Thus, it's important to find out what your sabotaging belief might be. Here's where a trusted spiritual coach can help. There are processes you can use to get to the core belief that has been hindering your progress, and sometimes it helps to know what the originating cause of that belief is. But it is not always necessary. In the final chapter of this book, I'll introduce you to the Fear to Faith process created by Lloyd Strom and Marcia Sutton. This is one of the most impactful and life-changing tools I've ever used. I use it with most of my coaching clients.

Most of the time, the best way to go about changing what you are feeling and thinking is to put your minds off what you don't want and on what you do want. You can't think two contradictory thoughts at the same time. You can't, for instance, stand up and smile and cry out, "I feel great and I feel awful!" (If you don't believe me, just try it.)

Changing your focus is simple—but you have to practice it! Someone who plays Beethoven's music well, for instance, makes it sound so easy. It is—once the musician has practiced and practiced and practiced.

If you've spent years thinking a particular thought and having a particular feeling, it may take a while before you can recognize the negative thought and shift beliefs. For example, I used to think that to grow, it was important to be corrected continually. You can imagine what that brought into my life. People were always telling me what they saw wrong and how I could fix it. Because of this belief, I kept attracting people who would find fault and criticize many of the things I was doing or saying.

When I realized that this belief was running my life, I began to notice how many subtle ways it showed up. It didn't change all at once. Each time I noticed it happening, I would release the belief that something was wrong. I finally decided to replace the need for correction with the acceptance of compliments. Gradually, what people began saying to me changed. When I changed my false belief, my experience began to shift.

This book is not about instantaneous manifestation of all you've ever wanted simply by thinking it so. It's about changing your internal focus and practicing new beliefs until they become second nature. And when we practice what is natural, it becomes easy. You've got to be willing to let it be easy.

As you read on, you may find out that the answers you've been looking for are very simple. Truth and wisdom are often expressed in simple terms. Many people believe that life has to be hard in order to work. (This is a good belief to use the Fear to Faith practice on, as we'll discuss later.) Be careful not to dismiss the important truths you are about to contemplate just because they seem so simple. Life really is simple, but we make it complex.

What we focus on increases. It's simple, it's subtle, and it works when we learn how to focus.

So, in order for this book and this system to work for you, you have to accept some truths about yourself.

You are magnificent! You have inherited all that you need to live your life to the fullest potential. Having a fully functioning, easy life, fully expressing yourself is natural. It's what you've been made for. You know that, don't you? If you didn't, then you wouldn't be longing for things to be different than they are.

There's an innate call in all of us to *be* more than we currently are, to *do* more in life or to *do* things differently, and to *be* all we can be. If these words just don't ring true, then perhaps this book is not for you. This message can only be applied by those who are willing to look *at* and *for* the good, beginning with themselves. If you are willing to start there, seeing the good within yourself, then you have taken the first step on the road to experience all the good there is for your life.

A number of years ago I read a pamphlet called *The Golden Key* by Emmet Fox. In essence it said, stop thinking about the difficulty, whatever it is, and think about God instead.[3]

I loved what Emmet Fox said; and while it sounded right, I found myself (and others to whom I have taught this message) puzzled about just how to do that. The key to life, according to Fox, is essentially to keep our minds off our problems and put them on God.

I liked that idea and began to try it. But at the time it was too nebulous. When I had a problem—a bill I couldn't pay, or an illness that wouldn't heal—it was pretty challenging to just think about God. I tried, trust me. But the concept of God was just too tenuous for me to grasp at those moments.

When your thoughts are unproductive, when problems or difficulties seem larger than life, it's pretty hard to think about God. In fact, many have said to me, "God? I just don't believe right now, so how can I think about God?" I've been attempting to find ways to teach this ever since. The answer to all our worries and desires in life is to understand who God is and who we are as well.

Twelve Qualities: The Divine Dozen

At a Sunday service, a teacher of mine gave me a sheet of paper with twelve qualities written on them—the same qualities you'll see in the next chapter of this book. She suggested we choose a quality and begin to look for more of it in our lives.

I did just that. When I focused on joy in life, more joy seemed to show up everywhere. When I decided to focus on order, I wasn't quite prepared for what happened at the time. Everything unlike order began to show up first. I saw all the places in my life that were "out of order." Even things like electrical equipment that had worked perfectly before began to fail. I learned an important lesson: this stuff takes time. The internal acceptance of a divine quality must be firmly rooted for the externals to change.

Often, when you have focused on the negative, however unconsciously, and then begin to focus on what you really want rather than what you don't want, more of the opposite shows up *at first*. But then, if you stick with the new focus long enough, things begin to change around you.

When this happened to me, I began to pay closer attention to the ancient wisdom teachings that say that what we focus on increases or that which we resist, persists. The reason that it persists is that it's what we are giving our attention to. So, I invite you to try an experiment.

What would your life be like if, this year, you chose one of the Divine Dozen and gave it your full attention? That means you read about it, you think about it, you carry and wear symbols that represent it, you put signs around your home or office to remind you of it, and you speak about it. You let it consume you—the way you used to let what was missing consume you. Can you see how this would change your internal awareness of who you are? And the more you own the divine quality in you, the more you will attract what you want.

I started by focusing on different qualities for a day at a time, and then a week at a time. Now I've decided to get the maximum benefit from this practice, so I've chosen a quality to focus on each year. Don't worry that the focus will be too narrow; focusing on any one quality actually enhances all of them, since Go(o)d can't be divided.

A few years ago, for example, I decided to focus on abundance. How do you focus on abundance and not begin to see places where you lack? By developing an attitude of gratitude that says *there is always enough*. To help me do this, I started the practice of writing one hundred things for which I was grateful every single day. What a difference that made in my life! I found myself going through my days wondering what I would write about the next day, so it kept me looking for things for which to be grateful. Even when something

unpleasant happened, I found something to be grateful for in the process. It was amazing. I've kept up an abbreviated version of this practice. Now, every day, my mastermind partner and I send each other
an e-mail with five things we are grateful for as we begin our day. It's
awesome!

Someone came to see me last week and said, "Toni, I've been looking at my life. I don't like where I've been the last few years. I haven't
accomplished anything. I don't have the money I wanted to have
saved. I just ended a relationship that I thought would lead to a long-
term commitment, and my business and career are failing." He went
on and on. Then he began to say, "I need to be more disciplined. This
coming year, I'm going to …" He proceeded to tell me how he was
going to fix all his problems.

As he spoke, I saw such sadness in his eyes, and his words were so
self-condemning. I could hear the shame and blame he felt the whole
time he was speaking. I knew his resolve would never last. The goals
he was setting were based on lack and limitation. While it seemed
laudable that he wanted to make progress in his life, and that he was
making an honest assessment of the things he wanted to turn out differently, he was focused more on the problem than on the solution.

Can you see what's wrong with this approach? Fix problems.
That's what most of us attempt to do with New Year's resolutions—and often with goals—and that's why they don't work.

Nothing about our lives is broken, and nothing needs to be fixed. If fixing things is where your thoughts are, I can guarantee you'll land in a mess of trouble. We are not broken toys in need of fixing; we have within our essence everything we need, and we know how to use that power if we make any resolution today.

You may already be seeing the quality that is calling out to you.

Keep your mind focused throughout the day on all the positive aspects of your life. Do you put your attention on the qualities or essence, or is it focused on worry, criticism, and fear? Keep looking for a new way of seeing things and you will experience a new way of being.

I asked the man who came to me last week what he felt drawn to experience more of during the coming year. "Order," he replied, without a moment's hesitation, and then laughed. "Every time I looked at the list of qualities in the past, I bypassed order, because I kept seeing it as something I had to do and don't do well. Today, I see it differently."

These twelve qualities are not "to do" lists; they are who God is. They are who we are, the very nature of our existence. Therefore, they are more about *being* than they'll ever be about *doing*.

You already possess these qualities; you just may not be using them as fully as you could be. When you begin to accept them and live them, you will have all the things you've wanted. We are made in the image and likeness of God. Most of us realize by looking at our parents or our children that the apple doesn't fall far from the tree. This is true spiritually as well. We inherit all of the qualities of God, because we are individualized expressions of God.

The system I present here is about learning to focus on the innate qualities of our being. Sometimes these qualities are covered over with fear or doubt or habits; but as you go through this book you will discover and own the truth that everyone innately possesses each of these qualities.

It feels so much better to focus on Go(o)d, doesn't it? Think about this for a moment. Consider a goal you may have right now, such as being in a relationship. I've counseled numerous people on this one issue alone. They start by writing down the list of qualities they want in a partner, and they look at the list daily. They visualize themselves in relationship and, sure enough, someone enters their life. Weeks later they come to me and say, "I forgot to put *XYZ* on the list; it's missing. I'm finding that this person brings out *QRS* in me, and I don't like it. I'm not sure I can commit. I'm not sure this is the right person. Remind me why I wanted a relationship in the first place. Maybe I'm better off alone."

Imagine, instead, that when people decide that it is time for partnership and love in their lives, they begin to focus on the love that they already possess. They start asking such questions as, "How would I act in this situation if I were truly loving?" They do things differently than before. They begin practicing loving themselves more and looking for ways that they are already in partnership, in cooperative efforts with others.

Then, when love comes along for a couple, it's not something outside themselves. It's the mirror of *who they already are*. That makes all the difference. Having someone in your life who can love you and whom you can love isn't the answer. *Being* the one who can have love and give love is!

Whenever you think of something you could use more of, start by being more of it and giving more of it, and you'll be amazed at the way your outer world begins to reflect your inner dimension.

Life, after all, is an inside-out job, not the other way around. When we focus on who we are *being*, the *doing* follows naturally, and then the *having eventually* comes along.

Practice

In the next chapter, we'll talk about what the different divine qualities are and how to choose one. In the next two chapters, you'll get a taste of two of the qualities you already possess, abundance and beauty, and you'll find ways of being with those qualities. At the end of this book, I'll give you an affirmative prayer that you can repeat every day, as well as Web sites through which you can learn how to write your own affirmative prayers.

If you visit my Web site, www.tonilamotta.com, you'll find many products and ideas to support you as you practice your focus. And you'll have so much fun in the process! This system lets you enjoy the practice. It's not about hard work. It's not about *doing* a lot of things in order to become something.

Instead, it's about letting yourself be your best and highest self. It's about loving and accepting the fullness of you. It's natural.

I also recommend that you read books about your chosen quality. From time to time, I'll recommend books on the blog as well as on my personal Web site, www.tonilamotta.com.

If you are a slow reader, read at least four books during the year. But if you really want to see the quality expand in your life, read a book at least once a month on the quality that you choose. The results you'll begin to see will amaze you.

Choosing and being a quality takes a commitment to continually unfolding and growing. It takes daily practice of owning your highest self for the rest of your life. It will help to read this book several times; the ideas will seep into your subconscious mind, and you'll even begin to notice when the goals you have set encourage you to think about what you don't have instead of what you already possess.

But in order to get the most out of this book, you'll need to stay tuned to the ongoing focus on your quality. Find other people who are focused on the same thing. Start a joy club, for example. You can find some already started if you search the Internet for a laughter club in your area. Many of them meet regularly and have different laughing exercises. Imagine the fun you could have with this! And know that transformation will occur.

You won't become something you aren't, but you'll get to live more fully who you already are. It's not a matter of achieving more, learning more, or getting better. It's a matter of simply remembering the truth about yourself. You are made in the image and likeness of God. The qualities that you know are true about God are, therefore, also true about you. You need only to claim them as your own.

So I invite you begin to choose a quality and give your full focus and attention to it. Wear things that remind you of the quality. Keep signs around. Talk about it. Read about it. Ask yourself how one who is experiencing this quality fully in his life might behave in this situation.

Your spiritual DNA can be molded into anything you choose. It is ready to encompass everything, because it is infinite. It is not a question of its willingness or its ability. It is entirely a question of your own receptivity.

Are you ready to receive?

Chapter 2
The Divine Dozen

In order to understand this Spiritual System for Success, it is necessary to understand two important things:

• Who is God?

• And who are you?

Almost all religions teach that God is One. Many describe God as both a presence and a power that is everywhere equally present. It is impossible for us to define God, for as it says in the opening of the *Tao Te Ching*, "The Tao that can be told is not the eternal Tao. The name that can be named is not the eternal name." [1]

All traditions teach that God expresses God-self as certain qualities or attributes. The most common of these is that God is love. But the truth is that God is also peace, power, beauty, and order.

These qualities are the essential nature of God; these qualities are therefore the essence of our nature. It doesn't matter whether you believe that you are made in the image and likeness of God, are a child of God, or, as I do, that you are made of the same God-stuff. As a drop of the ocean is not the whole ocean, it is holographically the ocean; for in it is contained all that the ocean contains. Similarly, we inherit the same qualities that we attribute to this infinite, divine nature.

When we accept this idea, *truly* accept this idea, we come to recognize our true nature. Once we recognize our true nature we can then welcome the expression of these qualities throughout all parts of our life. Then we will be living the life of grace/goodness/God.

These divine qualities are our natural state; indeed, they are our inheritance.

There is no limit to that which is infinite. There is no limit to beauty, peace, power, abundance, balance, freedom, love, unity, wholeness, wisdom, joy, and order. Therefore, there is no limit to our expression of these qualities as well. (The only limits that exist are the limits we put on ourselves.) These are the twelve qualities I will discuss in this book. At some point I may add to this list; and if you choose a quality not described here, feel free to apply these principles to any quality you attribute to the infinite, to your good, and thus to yourself.

You can also get an audio (CD or MP3) of each of the other chapters by going to www.tonilamotta.com and clicking on the products page.

For now, I recommend that you choose a quality from the list below that resonates with you. This is step one in beginning to apply this system to your life.

Carefully read the following list and see which one of these qualities is beginning to choose you:

Abundance Plentifulness, profusion, ample or overflowing. The state of having more than enough.

Balance Equilibrium and harmony, an aesthetically pleasing integration of elements; enough energy and time to do everything that is important to you.

Beauty Loveliness, the quality in a person or thing that gives pleasure to the senses or pleasurability that exalts the mind or spirit.

Freedom Liberation, independence, ease. The absence of necessity, coercion, or constraint in choice or action.

Joy Delight, gaiety, bliss. A state of happiness; the emotion evoked by well-being, success, good fortune, or the expectancy of good.

Love The self-givingness of God to its creation. Affection, devotion, unselfish concern that freely accepts another and seeks his or her good.

Order Regular or harmonious arrangement and organization; a straightening out so as to eliminate confusion.

Peace A state of tranquility or quiet; freedom from disquieting or oppressive thoughts or emotions; harmony in personal relations.

Power Possession of control, authority, or influence. The physical, mental, or spiritual ability to act or produce an effect.

Unity Oneness, accord, continuity, without deviation or change.

Wisdom Knowledge, insight, good sense. The ability to discern inner qualities and relationship.

Wholeness The state of being complete, perfect, restored, unhurt, healed. Having all parts or components.

Have you chosen a quality to focus on? If so, then choose a period of time to focus on that one quality. Will you focus for a day, a month, a year using the tools provided?

If no quality jumps out at you immediately, or if several of the qualities are vying for your attention, then let me suggest some proven ways to help you choose a quality to focus on.

Do not—and I emphasize this—do not look at what you think may be lacking in your life and choose the opposite so that you can fix your problem. Hopefully, you can see by now that that would be focusing on what you don't have. Remember, the more power you give to lack, the more lack you experience.

A few years ago, I heard a talk given by Dr. Michael Beckwith in which he said, "Lack of evidence is not evidence of lack." I love that statement. It succinctly says what I am emphasizing here.

You experience in your life whatever you give your attention to. So if you are paying attention to say, not wanting to be ill any more, you will not be able to reach your divine quality of wholeness. If you focus on what you don't know and constantly tell yourself, "I don't know what to do," or, "I don't know how to do that," you have kept yourself from accepting your divine quality of wisdom. You cannot speak of war, believing that violence is more prevalent than harmony, and expect your world to be at peace.

You are that powerful.

You control what you experience. And your focus—especially your words and your emotion-filled thoughts—determine what you experience.

The evidence in your life, then, is not evidence of what is true, but of whatever it is you believe. People who don't believe things can change are destined to experience the status quo. We get in life what we expect, not necessarily what we think we deserve. We get in life what we believe life can give us and have faith will happen. Faith requires that in spite of what we see, we *know* that another truth is possible.

The process of selecting a quality to focus on is part of the focus. How do you feel as you read each quality? Do you find yourself saying, "I don't experience that one" or, "I only wish that were true"? It might not be the choice that is choosing you. You are still looking at these as goals to achieve rather than qualities to uncover and reveal.

Instead, find the quality that makes your heart sing. The secret of having everything you want in life lies in allowing yourself to know it is already yours. The way to get there is to notice how you are feeling and look for ways to expand the good feelings. What thought would make you feel good? What quality makes you smile and say, "Yes, that one is something I can feel and know and focus on and allow to expand in my life"? Choose the one that easily resonates with you, rather than the one to which you think you should be paying more attention.

Let the one you know is your truth, but may not be fully experiencing at the moment, choose you. What is the quality you can see yourself more fully expressing? What is the quality that calls to you and makes you say, "I am that"? That's the one with which it would be best to start.

You may decide to choose a quality each year, and so you will have a twelve-year growth plan. Imagine where your life would be if you did this!

Or you may decide to focus on one quality a month as a warm-up experience, and then repeat the list for each year of the succeeding years. Do whatever feels best for you, and keep focusing on the quality that supports you in growth until you feel like it is solid in your life.

I suggest keeping your focus for at least a month. Research shows that it takes at least twenty-one days to fully change a habit; so focus on each quality at least that long. Not living that quality is just a habit we have gotten into and one we can break as we begin to believe that the qualities are our truth rather than their opposites.

Go back now and read over the list. If you find yourself saying, "I need that," or feeling bad when you read a quality, that's not it.

If it would help, go back and read the first few chapters again before you move on.

When you are ready, get into a comfortable position. Close your eyes and go within. Now do whatever technique you have developed to quiet your mind and your body. Take a few deep breaths; play some soothing music; repeat a mantra. Do whatever it takes to center yourself.

After a few minutes, think about what it feels like to love unconditionally. Think of a time you felt that unconditional love, whether you were the one giving it or the one receiving it.

Sit in the feeling and presence of this love for as long as you want.

Now begin to ask these questions:

- Which of these qualities most resonates with me right now?

- Who am I at my core?

- What is my true essence and which quality will encourage me to bring that forth?

- Is this quality something I think I need to have fixed in my life, or is it something I can know is already mine?

- Which of these qualities puts a smile on my face and a song in my heart?

- Which quality would I love to surround myself with reminders of?

- Which quality could I hear other people say of, "Oh, yes, that's who he/she is?"

- What is my heart longing to express more of?

- What does my life wish to become?

- Where does my passion lie?

Once you have picked the quality, read out loud the prayer found in the last chapter of this book. Then hear, see, and feel what happens. You'll know. You always do!

Chapter 3
Abundance

"I am enough."

The way I like to define abundance is "the state of having more than enough." Does anyone ever feel as if he has more than enough? More than enough bills maybe, and more than enough worries, and more than enough to do; but many of us live as if scarcity were the law of the universe.

Just the opposite is true. We live in an abundant universe. But somehow, we have inherited some myths about scarcity. Where do they come from?

Maybe when we were told to share as children, we interpreted it to mean that there is not enough to go around. Have you been living with that feeling since childhood? When we see our world as deficient, then everything reflects that belief. What we see in life is what we get.

In order to begin seeing abundance, we need to replace the scarcity mentality with *sufficiency thinking*. I like the word *sufficiency*: just enough, not too much and not too little; enough to enjoy life, and enough to have all our needs and wants met. The question to reflect on, then, is, "Do I know what would be sufficient for me? What would be not too much or not too little, but exactly what I need?"

We also need to be careful of the myth that prevails in our society that "more is better." We live in a competitive culture of accumulation. We seem to constantly strive for a goal in a race that will never end. We're always striving for more.

No sooner do we get that goal than we immediately want the next thing, and then the next thing. When we always focus on the next thing, we miss the glory of this moment. When we buy into the promise that more is better, we can never arrive. We can never "be there." There is always something out there, just beyond us that we haven't reached yet.

How much of what we have in life is what we need or want? How much of it is simply a result of impulse, or a quick fix for something else that is lacking in our lives? Look around you. Think about the things you have accumulated. Think about the ways you see a lot of abundance in your life and ask, "When is enough, enough? Do I have enough? What would that look like for me?"

Toothless Grin is a great story that perfectly illustrates this point. It's set at Christmastime, but the message is timeless:

I was doing some last-minute Christmas shopping in a toy store and decided to look at Barbie dolls for my nieces. A nicely dressed little girl was excitedly looking through the Barbie dolls as well, with a roll of money clamped tightly in her little hand. When she came upon a Barbie she liked, she would turn and ask her father if she had enough money to buy it. He usually said "yes," but she would keep looking and keep going through their ritual of "do I have enough?"

As she was looking, a little boy wandered in across the aisle and started sorting through the Pokemon toys. He was dressed neatly, but in clothes that were obviously rather worn, and wearing a jacket that was probably a couple of sizes too small. He too had money in his hand, but it looked to be no more than five dollars or so at the most.

He was with his father as well, and kept picking up the Pokemon video toys. Each time he picked one up and looked at his father, his father shook his head, "No."

The little girl had apparently chosen her Barbie, a beautifully dressed, glamorous doll that would have been the envy of every little girl on the block. However, she had stopped and was watching the interchange between the little boy and his father. Rather dejectedly, the boy had given up on the video games and had chosen what looked like a book of stickers instead. He and his father then started walking through another aisle of the store.

The little girl put her Barbie back on the shelf, and ran over to the Pokemon games. She excitedly picked up one that was lying on top of the other toys and raced toward the check-out, after speaking with her father. I picked up my purchases and got in line behind them. Then, much to the little girl's obvious delight, the little boy and his father got in line behind me.

After the toy was paid for and bagged, the little girl handed it back to the cashier and whispered something in her ear. The cashier smiled and put the package under the counter.

I paid for my purchases and was rearranging things in my purse when the little boy came up to the cashier. The cashier rang up his purchases and then said, "Congratulations, you are my hundredth customer today, and you win a prize!"

With that, she handed the little boy the Pokemon game, and he could only stare in disbelief. It was, he said, exactly what he had wanted!

The little girl and her father had been standing at the doorway during all of this, and I saw the biggest, prettiest, toothless grin on that little girl that I have ever seen in my life. Then they walked out the door, and I followed close behind them.

As I walked back to my car in amazement over what I had just witnessed, I heard the father ask his daughter why she had done that. I'll never forget what she said to him.

"Daddy, didn't Nana and PawPaw want me to buy something that would make me happy?"

He said, "Of course they did, honey."

To which the little girl replied, "Well, I just did!" With that, she giggled and started skipping toward their car. Apparently, she had decided on the answer to her own question of, "do I have enough?"[1]

Abundance is a quality of God and a quality of the universe. We certainly can see that in nature. Try counting the blades of grass, the stars in the sky, and the grains of sand on a beach. Have you noticed that no matter what you think you'll never have again in your life, *more* always shows up?

I used to live in New York and loved Broadway shows. I went to see them all. The month before I went into a convent at age seventeen, my mom and I went to every show imaginable, because I thought I'd never see one again. I've seen numerous shows since. We give up things and think we'll never have them again. That's seldom, if ever, true. There's always more.

I once read that there are enough building materials for every person on this planet to have an estate, and enough food to feed everyone three times over; but these resources are not distributed properly. There is not a lack in the universe. Where, then, must the discrepancy be? Are you wondering, "Why don't I have my share?" By now, you know the answer: it's in your *thinking*. So, let's focus now on how to think abundance.

I would venture to say that there is some area of your life where you could use a boost, and you might even need a major overhaul. Stop and think of something that you may want that you think is currently missing in your life. Got it? It may be health, money, a relationship, a new car, or a new house—whatever comes to mind when you ask yourself what's missing in your life.

All the books on prosperity that I have read say the same thing: everything that manifests in the physical world first starts with a desire. We've got to get clear on what it is we want, and then when we ask, it is always given. If you are saying, "I don't know," well, then, no wonder nothing shows up. It can't show up if you don't know. You need to get very clear on what it is you want.

A lot of people don't want to want, because if they want and they don't get, they think they will feel worse. So they shut off all the wanting. They don't believe the universe is abundant; so, if they don't want anything, they will never be disappointed.

The universe mirrors back to us what we think and feel on a consistent basis, so it behooves us to get very clear about what we want. If nothing comes to your mind, if you think you have everything, then consider world peace. What you think you'd like more of doesn't have to be about accumulating things for yourself. If you get clear, it is always given.

Not so, you say? "I think I'm clear, and I'm not getting it." Well, the kind of asking I'm describing here—"Ask and you shall receive"—is not just the asking we do with our words or even our well-intentioned prayer requests. I'm talking about hidden or vibrational asking. We all have an energy, a vibration that constantly sends out messages to the universe. What I am receiving in my life at this moment is *exactly* what I am emotionally—although probably not consciously—asking for. What I am experiencing in my life is the emotional, vibrational, and energetic match to what I most deeply believe in my life. That's the truth. It's the law. The trick is to get into energetic balance with what you'd really like to happen, not necessarily what is happening.

Whenever we have a desire in life, all the forces of the universe rush to answer our request. There is a nonphysical substance from which everything that exists in this universe is formed, and the formation is the result of our thoughts and desires. That's the basic principle of all creation. Everything is created out of the "nothingness," out of the nonphysical substance and the force of our desire. So we create whatever we give our attention to.

In biofeedback, when a person gives attention to his cold hands with the intention of warming them, blood and energy flow to the hands. If you study exercise physiology, you learn that in order to exercise a particular muscle, you have to think about the muscle you are using, and that's part of the energy that lets you exercise that muscle.

We need to recognize this power of attention. When we give our attention to something, we are recognizing its potential. Would you look at a baby who cannot walk or talk and think that he's never going to walk or talk because he isn't currently doing it? Of course not. That's not the thing we look at. The potential of walking and talking is in the infant.

So, too, you must not think of yourself as being without something just because there is no immediate evidence of it. Start to notice what you are saying about what you are not currently demonstrating in your life. How many ways are you telling yourself it's never going to happen? Be careful what you are saying; this is really important. What you say reveals what you think and feel, and if you don't think something can happen, it can't.

We know that God is omnipresent—present everywhere in its entirety, at all times and in all places. I had a student who once in Dr. Seuss-like fashion said, "There is no spot where God is not." So it follows that all of this universal God force, source energy, is present wherever we center our attention. Where attention goes, energy flows and results happen.

Here's the key. Whether our attention is on what we want or what we don't want, the universe always says "yes." So if we spend time thinking about what we don't want to happen in our life, guess what? The universe says, "Yes!" We can have exactly what we are focused on—what we don't want!

We spend a lot of time thinking about what looks like our goals, the things we think we want in life. We focus on what we don't have and we say, "I'd rather have that than this. I'd rather be there than here. That's where I really want to be."

We may even get emphatic: "Let me explain. I don't like being here. It's really not my fault that I am. I don't know why I am. It's probably my parents, the set of genes that I've got, or maybe my karma." I've heard this a lot in my counseling sessions, and I've heard it a lot in my own head.

Isn't that what we do? We spend more time focused on what isn't so, which creates even more of what isn't so. Why do we get what we don't want? Because we spend time saying we don't want "it," whatever "it" is.

Neuro-Linguistic Programming teaches us that the mind doesn't hear negatives, such as, "I don't." The universe doesn't hear "I don't"; it only feels the energy behind your intention. So, if you are spending all your time worrying about your health, your bills, or your love life, and thinking about what you don't have, you are actually creating more of the same. You are really good at creating; you've got to understand that.

Whatever is manifesting in your life is exactly what you have been focusing on. That's why you are creating exactly what you have. So understand how good you are at creating what you are thinking and feeling, because when you understand how good you are, then you can change what it is you are focused on.

At times we justify saying, "I want that because this hasn't worked for me. I don't like it." Do you see what is happening? All of our attention is on what we don't want; so the energy is flowing to what we don't want, and that's what we create more of.

This doesn't make rational sense, but it is exactly what we do. How much of your day do you spend seeing and knowing the truth of what you want? And how much of your day do you spend seeing and worrying about the things you don't want in your life?

The anticipation of lack, of not having enough for anything you need or earnestly desire, tends to create the circumstances of lack and "not enough."

Watch what you say as well. People continually say to me, "I said it, but I didn't really mean it." Guess what? Your unconscious spoke. You did mean it, the you that is the deepest part of you. So watch what you say. Your words reveal your thoughts. When you affirm lack or limitation, as in, "I can't afford it" or, "I can't do or have or be something," or, "It can't happen to me," the impersonal law will produce on demand more lack or limitation. We get in life whatever we believe.

We experience abundance when we take our focus off of lack and limitation. In his book *Communion with God*, Neale Donald Walsch tells us that the first illusion in life is that need exists, and that all the other illusions are created because of this. Need does not exist in the mind of God. God has created everything that is going to be created. It's simply ours to allow it.

He writes, "Abundance is not created as a result of certain conditions. Certain conditions are created as a result of Abundance. Happiness is not created as a result of certain conditions. Certain conditions are created as a result of Happiness. Love is not created as a result of certain conditions. Certain conditions are created as a result of Love." [2]

Being precedes experience *and* produces it. In other words, your consciousness creates your experience. In order to experience greater prosperity, greater abundance, greater health, and more love, forget you don't have it. Forget you don't have everything that you need right now, because you do have it. In your being, in your presence, you are enough, and all is well. Recognizing this makes all the difference.

That's why so many teachers teach the power of visualization—seeing what pleases you and would make you happy—rather than what is. I heard Esther Hicks, an inspirational speaker who dialogs with a group of entities called Abraham, where she says that people often ask Abraham, "Shouldn't we be facing reality?" Abraham clearly asserts, "Never face reality unless your reality is just the way you want it to be."[3]

Wayne Dyer, author of *The Power of Intention*, agrees when he asserts, "Nothing is more important than that you feel good!"[4] His Holiness, the Dalai Lama agrees when he says, "I believe that the very purpose of our life is to seek happiness."[5] That goes against the teachings many people grew up with because it sounds selfish. We need to be selfish enough to be at one with our source and experience who we really are as abundance. Everything we could ever want or need has already been given. We don't have to beg God or continually repeat affirmations over and over trying to convince ourselves or someone else. The practice is to continually reach for the thoughts that feel good.

When you find yourself thinking things that worry you, when you find yourself thinking things that are setting up fear, ask yourself, "Does this thought feel good? Do I want to hold onto this thought?" If not, stop!

People say to me, "Toni, I don't know how to change my thoughts." I reply, "Think of the Statue of Liberty. Now, think of the American flag. Can you still see the Statue of Liberty? How did you do that? How do you change your thoughts? *You just change them.* You think of something else. See what you just did? Take your attention off one and put it on the other."

And, if your attention goes millions of times a day to what you don't have—to lack of health, lack of money, etc.—change your attention. Say, "No, I'm going to think about what it is that I choose to be creating and what it is that God/the universe/all that is/ has already given in this world, and I'm going to focus on that rather than on lack and limitation."

Look in life for what you want to see rather than what may be in front of you. Appreciate everything that is. You can't appreciate and resist at the same time.

Gratitude is the attitude that brings more good into our lives than anything else. Find ways to compliment rather than complain. Let in every possible reason to feel good.

This makes sense, doesn't it? Yet do we live it? We live more in worry, fear, doubt, anxiety, and all the other negative things, rather than simply continually changing our thoughts to be on things that would make us feel good.

Keep being grateful. I find myself looking each day at what I can be grateful for. I'm keeping a gratitude journal, so I spend the day finding things that I can write about in my journal on the next day. It's an interesting way to live. The spirit of gratitude is a positive affirmation that the gift has already been given. You cannot be in the spirit of gratitude and fear at the same time.

What can you be thankful for?

• For what I already have.

• For the opportunities that come to me. Millions of opportunities show up every day.

• For the avenues of our good that open to me.

• For what I don't have yet, but expect to manifest.

• For what I do have, that don't think I want.

So what is it that we are to be thankful for? Basically, for everything!

This week I got a flat tire and a speeding ticket. They weren't on my list of things I'd like to have more of in my life, especially the speeding ticket! I also didn't have my insurance card with me, so the ticket cost me almost $500. That hurt. My initial reaction was to well up in tears and feel bad and angry with myself for not paying more attention to what I was doing. I knew how to get the sympathy of the police officer.

But instead, I stopped myself and realized that getting a fine just meant more money was coming into my life. I had to find money in order to pay for the ticket. So, I could feel grateful. This was an opportunity to expect more abundance.

I'm serious! Whatever happens in your life that looks like a negative is simply an opportunity to say, "Hey, universe, there's a need here, come and fill it!" You can then feel grateful. It's great to practice this when something unexpected happens.

Stop and wonder—the awe kind of wonder, not the worry kind. And begin to observe how the universe will send you what you need. Whenever you think you have a need, stop and realize that you live in an abundant universe. It supplies everything.

Begin to wonder how the universe is going to handle this situation. Expect it to do so. That's the only way it will come. It always shows up. It may not show up in the way you think it's going to show up, because you stop and think, "It has to come from here. I only make *x* amount of money, and think it's going to come from any place else." Or, "I think *this* is the magic potion that is going to make me well, and it's really *that*." But when we expect things to be abundant, it's fun to see how the universe brings it to us. It's a great way of playing in the game of life.

There was a woman who longed to find out what heaven was like. Every day she would pray, "God, grant me a glimpse of paradise." She prayed for years, until one night she had a dream. In her dream an angel came and led her to heaven. They walked down a street until they came to an ordinary house. The angel pointed to the house and told her to go inside. The woman went into the house and found a person preparing supper, another reading the newspaper, and children playing with their toys. She was very disappointed and returned to the angel on the street. "Is that all there is to heaven?" The angel replied, "The people you saw in that house are not in paradise. Paradise is in them."

Did you ever wake up in the morning saying, "I wonder what good will happen today in my life"? It's a great thought to start your day with. And every time something good happens, you'll notice and say, "Hmm, I wonder if this is the good I was expecting today. This must be it. Flat tire? I must be getting good today." That's how you can practice expecting more abundance. It's not just in our moments of prayer when all is well and good. It's in the everyday life. Paradise is within us.

A friend once had to pay $100,000 in taxes one year. He was complaining when his accountant said, "Instead of complaining, you could realize that this shows you how much you made, and be grateful!" What a sobering idea—and the only way to increase abundance in our lives.

Be grateful for whatever comes into your life. It's constantly pushing you toward more good. That's its only purpose. We don't have a source that's saying, "I'm out here to make sure you fail. I want to see how good you are because I'm punishing you." Is that the God/universe you believe in? The one that says, "I'm never going to meet your needs. You? I made a mistake when I created you. I didn't mean you"?

What kind of God do you believe in? Expect the good.

Abundance is like oxygen—there's always more of it out there. We don't get the more by trying to hoard or worrying that we don't have enough. We simply let it flow. Have you ever sat on your front porch breathing in deeply in the morning because you thought maybe there was going to be less oxygen later? You know that there's always going to be more—constantly.

Once we have put forth a desire to the universe, we need to release it and not keep looking to see if it's here yet, worrying about when it's going to come. That would be like planting a seed and constantly digging it up to see if it has grown.

I had a novice mistress back in my convent days who used to say to me that my biggest problem in life was that I was building an incredible tapestry but that I kept turning it over to see how much I had done. "The more you keep turning it over," she said, "the slower it is to build it."

I never forgot this image. "Is it happening yet? Is it here yet? Did I get it yet?" That's what we do to ourselves. "I didn't get it yet. I've been praying for this for months." What are months in the eyes of the infinite? Shift your belief so that whatever it is you desire is already yours—because it *is* already yours! There is no past or future in God.

There is only now, and everything you ever desire or need is in that place. It's only a matter of allowing it.

Let me illustrate by paraphrasing a story I heard in a motivational presentation many years ago.

> A minister was spending a few days with a family who were members of her church. During dinner, the subject of conversation was faith. "Do you believe with the Bible that faith can move mountains?" asked the husband. "Yes, I do," the minister said calmly. "All right. Tonight I'm going to bed with the belief that the mountain facing our home will be gone in the morning," proclaimed the head of the household. The next morning he eagerly looked out of the window and, seeing the mountain still there, bragged, "I knew it wouldn't go away!"

How many times do you hear yourself say, "I knew that wasn't going to happen. I knew I wasn't going to get that job. I knew this wasn't going to work. I knew that wouldn't come anyway"? If you *know* it, why are you expecting it to be different?

In addition to gratitude and belief, forgiveness is essential to the quality of abundance. The truth is, God never forgives us. God doesn't ever see us as anything but a reflection of itself.

God knows that we are simply reflecting what we believe at all times, so there is no need to forgive. God is not looking for something we did wrong and waiting to punish us. God is seeing us as a reflection of itself, and is constantly holding us in that perfection.

But we often block the flow of abundance by counting our losses. We dwell on things that shouldn't have been, in our estimation. We fret over things—ours and others'—that we call mistakes. We would do well to consider that nothing is ever lost. Everything in life can be a springboard to greatness. Abundance is seeing things from God's point of view, and God never sees anything lacking or missing.

Ernest Holmes, paraphrasing Elbert Hubbard, a philosopher of the nineteenth century, aptly put it, "We are not punished for our sins but by them."[6] God doesn't punish us. God doesn't dwell on past mistakes. We shouldn't either. Whenever there is a lack of abundance, there is a lack of forgiveness. Forgive yourself. What you did can never be as bad as you are making it. Let the other person off the hook. He or she did nothing to you that you weren't inviting in, even though in most cases it is not a conscious invitation. Forgiveness opens the door to abundance.

Finally, in order to have abundance, we must know the source of all things. It's not our job or anyone else's job to figure out where abundance comes from. No one here is supplying us. It comes from source energy. What we must do is to imitate the source.

We need to be one with the source in order to experience the abundance. We know from physics that energy is never destroyed. One thing we know about God is that God is constantly creating, constantly becoming more of itself by giving of itself. We shall never know the true secrets of prosperity until we learn to give.

There is a Divine Law of Circulation. We live in a world of magnificent abundance. There is enough for everyone, and we receive most when we give most. If you want love, give love. If you want more harmony, be more harmonious. If you want more money, give more money. If you want more time, give of your time.

A story was told of a person who received one million dollars from an anonymous giver. Someone remarked, "Wow, I would like to be the person who received that million dollars." A wiser person said, "I'd like to be the person who can *give* a million dollars!"

Which are you? Which would you rather be? There are two types of people who walk into a room: one who says, "Hi! Here I am!" and the other who says, "Oh! There you are!"

Buddhism teaches that there are three kinds of givers:

- **Beggarly givers**. They give only after much hesitation, and then just the leftovers, the worst of what they have. The underlying belief is that there is not enough. "I'll give a little, but I have to be careful."

- **Friendly givers**. They give what they themselves would use. They share what they have and with less deliberation, with more open-handedness. The underlying belief is that there will always be more in a friendly universe. "I can afford to share."

- **Kindly givers**. The highest kind of givers, they offer the very best of what they have, never expecting a return. "I give because I love to give."

Do you give a person a present and then ask, "Why are you not wearing/using what I gave you?" It's the "I gave you that and I should be able to control what you do with it" mentality. That's an interesting way of giving gifts. "I'll give it, but you better be aware that I gave it to you and you better appreciate it, at the very least."

Kindly gifts are what we get from the source. They're given from the knowledge that there is more than enough. We are at our best when we are giving from abundance. If we give from "I don't have enough but I'll share it," guess what happens? We don't have enough. But when we give from a sense of abundance, more comes.

We are at our best when we feel the freedom of giving that emanates from a deep sense of abundance. At all times, the spirit from which we give will reflect the spirit in which we will receive. We are made to give. Abundance is not just about money. It's about all good things. It is freedom from fear, living a life of grace.

The universe is abundant. God is abundant. I am abundant. I have enough. I am enough.

Chapter 4
Balance

"There is a time for every purpose under heaven."

(Ecc.3:1)

Do you make time in your life for everything that is important to you? Notice I said *make*, not *have*, because we all have exactly the same number of hours in a day and days in a year. It's how we choose to use them that makes the difference.

The quality of God that we turn our attention to now is balance. Some people think they are in balance when they feel as if they have everything in control in their lives. Or, for those who are Libras, it's a constant desire to weigh and measure things to be certain they are coming out just right. That kind of balance reminds me of being on a teeter-totter when I was young. Remember that board on a triangle that was in almost every neighborhood park? When you and the other person were exactly even, it was no fun.

There is a difference between "spiritual balance" and a "balancing act." One comes from God's work within us to bring order and priority to our lives. The other relies on outside resources to organize our time and tasks.

We constantly put ourselves under the gun. In seeking to achieve balance in our lives, it's important to understand the difference. A balancing act is an outward attempt to meet the demands of the many responsibilities of our lives. We have to work hard, we have to do it all, and we have to make it all work. We think that in order to achieve balance we need to focus on organizing tasks, time, and responsibilities, becoming more organized and developing better time management skills. Isn't that what balance is about? No, that's a balancing act. The results of this type of effort are useful but have limited ultimate impact.

The true balance we need and desire is spiritual balance; something that comes from source, something we experience more of as we seek to know how to live in that energy more intimately. Balance as a divine quality focuses on *being* rather than *doing*, and reflects the real priority for our lives. We achieve spiritual balance as we diligently make knowing and trusting God/the universe/divine intelligence the priority of our lives each day.

Balance is not about having it all together, or nothing ruffling your inner or outer being. That's a nice goal in life; however, I'm not talking about things we have to work toward, but things we need to uncover because they are our natural tendencies. The divine qualities are our inheritance. They are who we are at core but who we sometimes forget.

I like to think of balance as the blending of seeming opposites in life. As we focus on source energy as a priority in life, we discover that there are no opposites; there is no duality. Yet in our experience, we see things that way all the time. (I discuss this more in chapter XII.)

For example, we label our experiences as ups and downs, and most of us want to spend most of our time feeling up. I once had a wise lawyer friend who told me that I could expect my business and my life to be just like a roller coaster, with all of its ups and downs. Actually, the down part of the roller-coaster ride is the most exhilarating if we learn to relax into it.

Most of us would like life to be a series of wonderful events one after another, with nothing happening that upsets or disturbs us in any way. Upsets in my own life have sometimes been the greatest vehicles for my spiritual growth, when I just let them be and learned what the healing was about. The reason these events are upsets is because we feel that there's something not in alignment with us. There's something that needs to be shifted. Any kind of upset in life can be seen that way.

The foundress of my former religious community, Mother Mary Veronica, was often known to say, "The best growing days are the days the sun does not shine." Spiritual growth in our lives doesn't come in the moments of calm. This may sound contradictory, but it's true. It doesn't come in meditation and in prayer. However, the moments of calm, the moments of meditation and prayer, teach us how to look at things that throw us off balance so we can glean the most from them.

If we don't let moments of meditation and prayer teach us through the upsets, then we start thinking that life is one upset after another. Our reaction to another difficulty is, "It's all those people out there. I've got to deal with this. What a mess!" Isn't this how we often react, rather than think, "Ah, another gift!" When we center our life in prayer and spend our life absolutely committed to God and to our spiritual growth, we see that the very things that are calling us to center are what seem to be throwing us off.

Did you know that an eagle knows when a storm is approaching long before it breaks? The eagle will fly to some high spot and wait for the winds to come. When the storm hits, it sets its wings so that the wind will pick it up and lift it above the storm. While the storm rages below, the eagle is soaring above it. The eagle doesn't escape the storm. It simply uses the storm to lift it higher. It rises on the winds that bring the storm. We can learn from the eagle.

I am also reminded that a jet plane spends 95 percent of the time in flight being off course, but gets to its destination by a continual process of slight corrections. That's what the pilot is there to do, constantly correct the flight. That's an apt metaphor for balance in our lives. Balance is not staying the course without error, but continual correction to come back to center. That's the true gift of balance.

While I was writing this chapter, I was on a retreat with a group of ministers at a Benedictine Abbey in Kansas City. We used the four elements of the Rule of St. Benedict as our focus for each of the first four days. Wouldn't you know that the first day was about balance! (There are no accidents in life.)

The exhortation was that we need a blending in life of work and recreation, inner and outer work, speaking and silence, and attention both to the physical and spiritual aspects of our lives. The harmonizing of these seeming opposites makes life work. How are you doing in your life with these aspects? Ask yourself how balanced you are in the area of work and recreation. Where do you spend most of your time? How about inner work and outer work? Do you live in the outer plane all the time and don't take the time you need for your inner life?

At the retreat we weren't in silence all day. I actually would have loved that. We did come together every morning and every evening but spent the bulk of the middle of the day in silence. It was a very profound experience.

I had the most profound experience of developing community that I've had in a long time. Thirty of us were there, but we left as one—most of that was because of the silence that we spent together. When we did come together to speak, we spoke out of a whole different depth because we had been together in silence. Our evening sharing times were rich with meaning. We also had time to sit with the monks, who were chanting the hours, or with the nuns. I received much healing that I didn't know I needed. (Life gives us gifts continually.) We all came together in the balance of talking and silence. We looked at that and started planning all of our future minister convocations around that idea. One year we'll go play and have fun, and the next year we'll choose to be back in the silence. Do you keep that balance in your life?

What about the physical and spiritual aspects of your life? Do you spend so much of your time in the physical realm that you neglect the spiritual? Or do you spend so much time in the spiritual realm that you neglect the physical? In the Order of Benedict, "Work and Pray" is their motto. Look at both of those things in perfect balance.

Many parts of our lives need to be brought into balance, and they may seem to conflict with each other: responsibilities to our families, the responsibility of earning a living, maintaining our health, giving attention to our spiritual lives, keeping up with the deluge of information required to function today, our duties to community or church activities, and the myriad of other demands on our time and energy.

Everywhere we look we can see people who are out of balance. There are people with heart attacks, people who live in so much stress because parts of their life are out of balance, or people who are ill because of poor eating habits and lack of exercise. There are people who live too much in their heads, who haven't integrated head and heart. There are spiritual giants who die agonizing deaths from an illness from years of denying or neglecting the body. No one of these things is better than the other. There are people so caught up in caring for their bodies, minds, and social lives that they never think about their spiritual nature. And there are people so caught up in their feelings that they neglect their minds, or fail to use their reasoning ability. They, too, have failed to integrate head and heart.

To balance all these aspects of our lives, we need something to balance them around, some point of equilibrium, like the teeter-totter. There is only one reliable point of balance, and that is God/source energy/life itself, that which pervades everything and underlies all the material and spiritual activities of life. We have to learn to make that our balance point. There is no other answer. When I look at life with clear understanding, it all boils down to this: balance means finding this source, and finding this is all about spiritual practice.

In our society, it's challenging to find time. I meet all kinds of retired people who never have time for anything. Think about that. When you are not working, you are not necessarily less busy. We need to find time to seek our center, so we have to simplify our lives;

there is no way around it. So much time is wasted in the endless pursuit of "newer and better" material possessions.

What is the result of our culture's obsession with material acquisitions? I remember once hearing something that I believe the Buddha once said: "Those who have cows have care of cows." The more we have, the more we need to care for. So take time today or sometime this week to do an analysis of your life: how much time do you put into caring for all the unnecessary "necessities"—the "toys" that the media and advertisements have made you believe you can't live without? There is nothing wrong with having material things, as long as they don't end up having you!

Time management classes teach you to record what you do every hour, so you can look at where you are *spending* your life. I recommend no less than an hour a day. If it is too hard to find an hour a day for spiritual practice, you are the kind of person who needs two!

What do you want to be remembered for? When I had my computer training business, I always went around saying, "Spirituality is the number one thing in my life." But you know what? I never took time for it. I was up at the crack of dawn to be in the office by 7:00 AM and I'd get home by 10:00 PM. Go home, go to sleep, and then get up. Pack a suitcase; go to the next client; run all over the world.

Who was I kidding? *Spirituality* was my top goal? It was out there somewhere, sometime, until I caught myself and said, "Wait a minute. I'm a liar." Those are pretty strong words, but it was true. I was a liar. I was saying that God/spirituality was the center of my life, but that's not how I spent my time. The measure of our balance is where we spend our time and where we spend our money.

I teach a Financial Freedom class created by Lloyd Strom and Marcia Sutton, and in it we complete a little chart that asks where our money is going. Where your money goes shows what's most important to you. And whatever you spend most of your time on shows what's most important to you. We must make sure that what we say is most important to us reflects in how we spend our time and money.

In addition to a specific time set aside for prayer and meditation, find ways to bring your awareness of source into your life every day as much as possible. At the monastery we were reminded by bells five times a day to pay attention to God. The monks call this practice "interruption." It suggests that even if you are praying, you should interrupt your prayer to remember God constantly during the day.

In Islam, Muslims take five times a day to turn toward Mecca and pray. I thought I could take that practice home by using the telephone—mine rings at least five times a day! We can use that continual reminder, the sound of the telephone, to bring our minds back to source. What would happen when you got on the phone? If not the phone, use something else to remind yourself of the center of your life. That will go a long way toward helping you keep your inner balance.

Ultimately, the secret of balance is to put God/source first. Paramhansa Yogananda, founder of the Self-Realization Fellowship, reminds us, "Giving God a second place is giving God no place."[1] Yet how often do we indeed give God second place—maybe third place, fourth place, eighth place, or tenth place? Somewhere we'll fit it in, because we feel everything else is more pressing. We continually delude ourselves with, "No, I have to do this; I can't afford to miss that." We end up putting off our spiritual practice, or forgoing it completely.

What I do when things get overwhelming is ask myself what three things I can knock off my list. It's always a challenge, because they all seem so important. What appointment could I cancel? What exercise could I cut out? What one thing am I doing that is keeping me so busy that I don't have time to be? How can I change that in my life? Discipline can help us overcome that "too busy" syndrome.

Schedule your life; plan a balanced routine of meditation so that you're getting a set amount every day, and then follow it. It's a matter of commitment. Should you fail on occasion, just try again. Persevere. When you make the determination, "I will do it, no matter what," you will see a wonderful change come into your life.

Have you noticed what happens when you promise a friend that you'll get together someday? But *someday* is not a day of the week. It just doesn't happen when you say you'll get around to it. "I know I want this in balance but ..." We need to commit to it and say, "I'm going to do a spiritual practice at 8 A.M., no matter what."

Doctors have proven that blood pressure and other bodily functions come into balance when we spend time daily in prayer. I probably have the lowest blood pressure of anyone I know. In fact, my doctor recently asked me, "How many hours a day do you meditate?"

How much time, how many days, do you spend during a month in silence? What a concept! Do you give yourself at least one day a month to focus on your spiritual life? That's like saying that God gets one out of thirty or thirty-one days.

Do you take at least a week one time a year, if not more, for a retreat to focus on your spiritual connection? I used to spend at least eight days a year in silence. Last year I went to the Oneness University in India, where I spent twenty-one days in silence. When I don't give myself silent time, I miss it.

Have you thought about spending a week out of every year just being with yourself? I enjoy my own company. Can you spend that time alone focusing on your spiritual connection? If you say that God is number one and that your spiritual life is your first priority, how well does your schedule show it?

Do you remember the scriptural commandment, "Remember the Sabbath day by keeping it holy" (Ex. 20:8)? I don't mean to be able to recite this commandment, but to remember to practice it. One day a week. We've lost that in our society. So many other things are now taking its place. Some people may get to spend an hour or an hour and twenty minutes, and even that seems long.

As we "remember the Sabbath," we will find that we are leading a much more balanced and healthy life—physically, mentally, and spiritually.

Suppose we give one day to committed spiritual practice. But what about the other six? When we speak of balance as a spiritual quality, we also speak of living life on purpose. As I said earlier, living in balance is having time to do everything that is important to you. Check out how you spend your life. Are you truly living and spending time on what is important to you? Do you even know what is important to you? What are the things that are most essential in your life? Are you spending time doing them?

For example, when did you take your last vacation? People tell me proudly, "I haven't had a vacation in three or four years." I want to know what's going on in your life. Are you seeing signs of burnout? When was the last time you took time to play? Making time for hobbies you enjoy is a necessary component of spiritual and psychological balance. You will get much more accomplished in your work and in your spiritual life, and you will be healthier physically if you remember this.

Steven Covey, in the *Seven Habits of Highly Successful People*, divides life into four quadrants.[2] Think about a grid, where across the top is Urgent and Non-Urgent, and along the side is Necessary and Not Necessary. We can categorize things in our lives as urgent and necessary, urgent and not necessary, not urgent and necessary, and not urgent and not necessary. Try it. Put the things you do in your life into one of those four quadrants.

When we are out of balance, much of our life is spent doing the urgent and not necessary. Are you a slave to your phone and e-mails, for example, giving them first priority in your life? E-mail was supposed to simplify our lives, but now I get 530 messages a day instead of five. Why do we do this? We make our first priority what someone else is calling to us, rather than what is coming from the center of our lives.

Most of us spend a lot less time on the not urgent but necessary—things like I'm suggesting in this chapter: figuring out what we really want in life and taking the time to examine how well we are doing with our life purpose. What if you really did all the things you have read about? I have seen a number of people who did, and what happened was a real life change. Will you allow yourself to take the time to do those things that are not urgent but oh, so necessary?

If you don't already have one, I suggest you spend time defining a vision for your life. What is it that you really want to accomplish while you are on this earth plane? Just getting by? Just making it through the day? You'll never know if life is in balance if you don't know why you came to this life.

Consider writing your own epitaph. What would you like to see written on your gravestone? What do you want said about you when you're gone? Perhaps you'd like yours to say, "A loving father and husband who always had time for us." If you want something like that on your gravestone, you aren't likely to get it if you're at the office seventy hours per week, and if you take your laptop and check your voice mail when you're on vacation. That is more likely to get you an epitaph that reads, "One of the world's most successful businessmen," or something similar.

There is nothing wrong with being a good businessperson, of course. But the question is, what is your vision for your life? What would you like to achieve before you die? What motivates you? What would you like people to say about you after you have gone?

My favorite "philosopher," the Cheshire Cat from *Alice in Wonderland*, once said, "If you don't know where you're going, any which road will get you there."[3] That's how many of us live our lives, following any which road. We let our lives just take us. We let our clients lead us—if I get fourteen calls, for example, I'll respond to them. Who's leading here?

We need to prioritize our lives so that we are spending time at work, at prayer, at play, on making life better for others, and on community building. No one thing should be exaggerated out of proportion to the other dimensions of life. Life is made up of many facets, and only together do they form a whole.

Many things call for our attention, and *all* of them have a place. We are called to live in harmony with life and to make time for the natural, the spiritual, the social, the productive, the physical, and the personal. Do you know the things you need to do to stay balanced? Your answer will differ from others. You may need to work more, or less. You may need to do more exercise, or less. You might need to listen to music or walk or participate in a sport. When was the last time you just sat down and listened to music? Do you take time for the things you most enjoy? It might be theater or a meal out with friends. It might be something you do as a ministry in church. Whatever it is, you need to make time for it. We all need a degree of variety in our lives.

Finally, to be truly balanced, you need to make room for love. We live in a society where people may be richer in many ways than ever before. Yet in the area of our relationships, we are poorer as a society than ever before. Many of us make little time for friends and family. I wonder how many parents read a bedtime story to their children, and how many families sit around the table for a family mealtime. Many of us have friends who live close by but whom we never take time to see.

Much of our interaction with other people now happens as we type brisk e-mails to each other. So many misunderstandings can occur when we communicate this way. Why do we do it? Because we don't have time to do it any other way? We don't have time to communicate, really communicate, with another person? As a result we live in a society where loneliness is endemic. To live a truly balanced life, we need to prioritize loving relationships and spend more time with one another. More than ever, we need to belong to a community in which real, honest, intimate relationships and communication are the norm.

Nothing is more important than our relationships. Our God is a relational God who calls us into relationship with each other. When I want to see the face of God, I need to look at the face of another person. It is in relationship that we truly come to recognize our life's purpose as well as to get to know God.

When we set priorities, relationships come first. To keep from burnout and to live in balance, we need God to be at the center of our lives. We get a vision for our lives as we prioritize accordingly, and as we seek variety and live lives of love.

Here is a summary of balance, using the letters of the word:

B—the blending of seeming opposites in life

A—all systems working together—physical, organizational, and personal

L—learning and living what is important in life, especially putting the first priority on relationship and love

A—acting on what may not be urgent but what is truly important

N—noticing what throws us off center and using those upsets to grow

C—constantly coming back to center

E—enjoying the roller coaster so much more

Balance is not about trying to control what happens, but allowing all of life to lead us to God. I am grateful for a life that continues to call me into balance, and I'm committed to enjoying the process. Are you?

Chapter 5
Beauty

"I love myself the way I am."

I had the privilege of being at the birth of a baby and she was handed to me right after being given to her mother. I held her and said, "We welcome you. You are beautiful. We are so glad you are here." As I write this, I have a mental image of babies being born all over the world, surrounded by people saying something similar to them. Wouldn't it be wonderful to be born to such a welcome? What a wonderful gift! I saw a bumper sticker once that said, "It is never too late to have a happy childhood."

In the 1995 movie *Don Juan DeMarco*, Johnny Depp was convinced he was Don Juan. He told Marlon Brando, his therapist, that the reason he was so attractive to women was because he saw the inner beauty of all women; and in his seeing it, they saw it in themselves and actually became beautiful. What power we have for one another!

Furthermore, what power we have for our whole culture, to change the way beauty is seen in our society. The simple act of recognizing beauty in another calls it forth.

In many of the classes that I teach, I play a song by Libby Roderick called, "How Could Anyone" (Ever Tell You, You Were Anything Less Than Beautiful). (You can find it at www.libbyroderick.com/cd_new.html). Almost everyone in the room is touched very deeply by this song. Perhaps because so many of us were given messages that made us feel anything but beautiful. In fact, most of the messages we heard from our families, our churches, our music, and the media tell us that we don't quite measure up. "You are a sinner and you are not worthy." "You'll never amount to anything." "You'll be a failure unless you buy this product."

I remember repeating the words, "Oh, Lord, I am not worthy," so often that I believed it. When we keep hearing something, after a while we believe it. Advertisements often tell us we are not good enough unless we use a certain product or have our teeth whitened or wear whatever is in fashion. It's subtle at times, but I realized long ago how I had been deeply influenced by these negative messages.

One year, when choosing a quality to focus on, I chose beauty. Or, I should say, beauty chose me. When I looked at the list, it jumped out at me and said, "Pick me, because it's time to truly see this in yourself." Perhaps my story will give you an idea of why.

Everyone has a signature story in life, and I am no exception. I grew up surrounded by all my Italian relatives. My best friend, other than my sister, was my cousin Terry, who happened to be a redhead. Everywhere we went, people would stop and look at her and say to or about her, "Isn't she beautiful?" As I stood next to her, I was convinced that I must be chopped liver.

On the other hand, people would look at me and say, "She's so smart." My cousin decided there and then that she must not be smart. Isn't it amazing how we make assumptions from the little bit we choose to hear?

No little girl wants to be smart; girls are supposed to be beautiful, right? I spent a good deal of my life trying to prove that I wasn't smart. Honestly! That's one of the reasons that I earned three master's degrees and two doctorates. I thought perhaps that somewhere along the line I would fail and then I could say to the world, "See, I'm not really smart."

Boy, was I confused. My cousin, on the other hand, never went to college, although she wanted to. Convinced that she was destined to use her beauty instead of brains, she married three times. I never did because I didn't think I was beautiful enough for anyone to want me.

One day in graduate school, I was upset and crying about something. I can't remember what it was about now. The head of the

Adult Education Department at Columbia University came over and put his hand on my shoulder and said, "I can't imagine why someone so smart and so beautiful could be so upset." Suddenly something clicked inside of me!

At that moment, I came to recognize that I had made smart and beautiful an either/or situation. It was as if this professor instantaneously wiped out years of pain. I immediately called my mother and told her what happened, and of course she said that no one ever meant that I wasn't beautiful, and added, "By now I hope you know you are beautiful." The erroneous beliefs we take with us throughout life are amazing.

Thank God that today I can now look myself in the mirror and sing, "You are so beautiful to me." In fact, I can't help but look at everyone I see and say the same thing. I'm amazed at how much beauty I now see.

Focusing on beauty as the divine quality of the year made an enormous difference for me because, as I've been saying, whatever we focus on increases. I see beauty in all the people I meet, and I see beauty in nature. I used to be oblivious to the beauty around me. (Growing up in the Bronx didn't help.) I think I've lived in my own thoughts for so long that I even missed seeing trees sometimes. Now I can notice the dewdrop on a leaf.

I even see the beauty in the circumstances of life that I previously would have called challenges. There's an exquisite beauty to the way life is ordered. You see, whatever quality you focus on, you get to focus on good instead of where you think there is a lack or limitation. You get to see infinite potential everywhere. You see harmony, order, beauty, and abundance, *everywhere*. Beauty is so much more than physical appearance, even though so much of our society is measured that way. It is in fact, the very image of the infinite in sensible form.

Most definitions of beauty place a lot of emphasis on externals. Most people spend most of their time looking at appearances as opposed to inner beauty. Stretch your knowing and recognize that to really understand beauty, you need to see not only appearances, but beyond appearances. Actually, that's how we get to understand the divine as well, because connecting to the divine is all about our ability to see beyond appearances.

What we are seeing and experiencing is only the tip of the iceberg, but sometimes we get caught up in that. If you've got ill health, sometimes that's all you see. If your relationship is not working, then that's all you see. Most of the time, we see whatever is happening in our lives as if this were the truth about life. We don't see beyond the appearance to the God beyond that. If you focus only on appearances, sometimes it doesn't look so good.

Likely you have heard the cliché that beauty is in the eye of the beholder. I encourage you to look with new eyes. Let's change pleasing to the "eye" that we see with to pleasing to the "I" who we are. We change beauty from what we see or look at with the senses to what we know as the truth of who we are. In this way, we behold our beauty.

Many years ago I read an article on the Body Shop Web site www.bodyshop.com that offered ten reasons why we should change the way we see ourselves and how to change society's image of ourselves. The article asked the following questions:

- How often is the person's appearance a reason that you admire them?

- What do you think are the most important attributes a person can have?

- What would you like another person to most admire in you?

Beauty is not how great you look. I don't know of anyone who is really complimented, deep down where it lasts, when someone says, "You look great today," or, "How pretty your red hair is." (I guess I'm still not completely healed!)

What we should look at is, what pleases us? Do we even know? What is beautiful to you? Scripture tells us, "Ask and it will be given to you; seek and you will find; knock and the door will be opened to you" (Matt. 7:7). Most of us don't even know what pleases us, what we want; and then we wonder why we don't get it.

So, what pleases you? What looks good to you? Be sure that your answer is not what everyone else tells you that you should have, or what society tells you is the measure of success, or what good looks are supposed to look like. What's really important to *you*? In his book, *The Prophet*, Kahlil Gibran said, "Beauty is eternity gazing at itself in a mirror."[1] When we focus on the quality of beauty, we behold our own beauty. If you only see with your senses, you'll miss so much of your own beauty and the beauty of life.

The English poet Percy Shelley once said, "Poetry lifts the veil from the hidden beauty of the world, and makes familiar objects be as if they were not familiar."[2] Whatever we look at, if we think we are seeing only what we are seeing, we are probably missing the reality. If all we see is what we see with our eyes, we are not *seeing* what we are not seeing.

So, the question is, "What eyes do you see with?" Is your life focused on what the senses tell you or what you sense beyond the senses? If something doesn't seem to be beautiful, ask yourself, why do I think it's not beautiful; and very shortly you may discover that there is no reason. A search for quotes about Beauty on Google, led me to one that was often repeated by the English painter John Constable who said, "I never saw an ugly thing in my life: for let the form of an object be what it may—light, shade, and perspective will always make it beautiful." [3]

So, what in your life can you now transform the view of? What are you seeing as less than beautiful? In what aspect of your life are you not seeing beauty that you can put a new light on, give it another shade, and transform the way it looks? You can do that.

Think of the Golden Gate Bridge in San Francisco (or any other bridge you may have seen recently). Now think of a herd of pink elephants coming in every door of your house. Can you still see the bridge while you are looking at the pink elephants?

While you are looking at one thing, you can't look at the other. That's how simple it is to change our thinking, to change our mind, to change what we focus on. We can do it; we all know how to do it. We do it all the time. In fact, the minute you attempt to meditate, doesn't your mind often go somewhere else? Your mind easily goes to something else. So why not choose to have it go elsewhere?

The American author, poet, and philosopher Ralph Waldo Emerson said, "Though we travel the world over to find the beautiful, we must carry it within us or we find it not."[4] Before we begin to see anything outside ourselves as beautiful, we need to work within ourselves and know that who we are is beauty. These are not clichés. We are the inheritors of all twelve qualities. We know that we inherit our family's traits, their qualities. I am my mother and my father. I am my grandmother and grandfather. I see so many of their characteristics and mannerisms in me. My father/mother, that which is, that which created the world and me, gives me its characteristics as well. So, if source energy/God is beauty, then that is who I am at my essence, at my core.

Now stay with this idea. Take a quality and sit in meditation knowing, for example, "I am beauty," and see what shows up. See what you see, and see what eyes you start to see with.

Children start becoming judgmental of physical beauty at an extremely young age. All the fairy tales tell us that the princess or heroine is absolutely beautiful, and the bad person or the witch is always ugly. To be good is to be beautiful. How confusing is that to a little child? "I can't be good!" What's going on here?

Kids fight to be included with the people who make up the "in crowd," who are often called "the beautiful people." Typically, these groups of popular kids shun anyone who doesn't match up to whatever standard of beauty they have set. Perhaps you wanted to be one of the beautiful people, whether it was the cheerleaders, the football team, or another group, because they were the ones whom everybody wanted to be like. But you did not fit in that crowd. Very few do.

Studies about how many teenagers suffer from anorexia and bulimia such as the ones listed in news-medical.net and family-firstaid.org, are frightening. Our society caters to the extremely beautiful, and the media do not help this situation at all.

Television constantly portrays beautiful people in shows, and in almost every commercial between shows. (Although this is beginning to change a bit in advertisements to become more realistic; thank you, Dove, for redefining real beauty.) It is virtually the same with magazines. The media are, and probably always will be, unless we do something or something drastic changes it, the biggest pusher of beautiful model-type people. If something or someone isn't seen as beautiful, reality programs show you how they can be.

Have you seen any of the shows about makeovers? Recently, there were more than fifteen "Oprah" shows alone about makeovers. You can have a room made over, a house made over, or your wardrobe made over.

Consider the popular show called "Extreme Makeover." The men and women on this show are not happy with their physical appearance, and they are set up with all kinds of doctors and makeover artists. These people make complete changes. They go through plastic surgery, liposuction, breast implants, and hair, makeup, and clothing changes. People have their faces and bodies cut up to alter themselves. They go through intense pain. The show reveals how much pain people have when they identify themselves with their form. At the end of the show, they often say that they have so much more self-esteem. And then their families recognize them more. It's frightening.

The popularity of those shows speaks of the resonance people everywhere have with the aspects of the fairytale archetype and the longing to be beautiful.

The Internet is filled with jokes about beauty. One such comes from BDWilliams.com:

> Little Johnny watched, fascinated, as his mother smoothed cold cream on her face. "Why do you do that, Mommy?" he asked.

"To make myself beautiful," she replied. Then she began to remove the cream with a tissue. "What's the matter," asked little Johnny, "are you giving up?"

We don't need cold creams, extreme makeovers, or face-lifts. What we need is a faith life! The faith that says, "I am that. I am beauty." You are beauty. He, she, or it is beauty. This too is beautiful. What if we practiced saying that all week with everything that happens? Can we see life as beautiful?

Albert Einstein once said, "The most beautiful thing we can experience is the mysterious. It is the source of all true art and all science. He to whom this emotion is a stranger, who can no longer pause to wonder and stand rapt in awe, is as good as dead: his eyes are closed." [5]

Can you fathom this? When was the last time you were rapt in awe and wonder? How many people walk around feeling rapt in awe and wonder? Most of us are rapt in confusion and fear, in "I can't do this," in, "What's going to happen?" What are you rapt in?

When was the last time you took time to notice something beautiful? Remember, whatever you focus on increases. Spend time each day noticing beauty around you, and let it touch you.

Helen Keller has been quoted as saying, "The best and most beautiful things in the world cannot be seen or even touched. They must be felt with the heart."[6] To cultivate the quality of beauty, you need to look beyond the physical but also take time every day to look at the physical as a starting place to begin to appreciate what lies beyond it.

As German playwright Johann Wolfgang von Goethe once said, "Hear a little music, read a little poetry, and see a fine picture every day of your life, in order that worldly cares may not obliterate the sense of the beautiful which God has implanted in the human soul."[7] That made me ask myself what I spend my time on. "Who has time to read a book, to listen to music, to go to a place of beauty?" That's the excuse people frequently give for not doing these things.

I hear more retired people today say that they don't have the time. "I'm too busy." What are we busy about? Take time to smell the roses. Can you, every single day, take time to listen to music, to read some poetry? What would life be like if you started living that way instead? To focus on what is real, what is important, what is beautiful, rather than what you now focus on, whatever that is. The moment that we give attention to anything, like a blade of grass, it becomes mysterious. It becomes awesome. It becomes a magnificent world unto itself. Take every opportunity to see anything that is beautiful, things like a sunset, a smiling child, or a flower opening in the morning.

If you truly love nature, you will find beauty everywhere.

I read a story that brought this message home to me. It's called "The Most Beautiful Flower" and I liked it so much, I got permission from it's author, Cheryl Costello-Forshey, to reprint it for you.

The park bench was deserted as I sat down to read

Beneath the long, straggly branches of an old willow tree.

Disillusioned by life with good reason to frown,

For the world was intent on dragging me down.

And if that weren't enough to ruin my day,

A young boy out of breath approached me, all tired from play.

He stood right before me with his head tilted down

And said with great excitement, "Look what I found!"

In his hand was a flower, and what a pitiful sight,

With its petals all worn-not enough rain, or too little light.

Wanting him to take his dead flower and go off to play,

I faked a small smile and then shifted away.

But instead of retreating he sat next to my side

And placed the flower to his nose

And declared with overacted surprise,

"It sure smells pretty and it's beautiful, too.

That's why I picked it; here, it's for you."

The weed before me was dying or dead.

Not vibrant of colors: orange, yellow or red.

But I knew I must take it, or he might never leave.

So I reached for the flower, and replied, "Just what I need."

But instead of him placing the flower in my hand,

He held it mid-air without reason or plan.

It was then that I noticed for the very first time

That weed-toting boy could not see: he was blind.

I heard my voice quiver; tears shone in the sun

As I thanked him for picking the very best one.

"You're welcome," he smiled, and then ran off to play,

Unaware of the impact he'd had on my day.

I sat there and wondered how he managed to see

A self-pitying woman beneath an old willow tree.

How did he know of my self-indulged plight?

Perhaps from his heart, he'd been blessed with true sight.

Through the eyes of a blind child, at last I could see

The problem was not with the world; the problem was me.

And for all of those times I myself had been blind,

I vowed to see the beauty in life,

And appreciate every second that's mine.

And then I held that wilted flower up to my nose

And breathed in the fragrance of a beautiful rose

And smiled as I watched that young boy,

Another weed in his hand,

About to change the life of an unsuspecting old man.

The Most Beautiful Flower

Chapter 6
Freedom

"I surrender to the process of co-creation."

There once were two construction workers who ate lunch together. Every day one of them would open his lunch box and exclaim in disgust, "Peanut butter and jelly again!"

Finally the other inquired, "Why don't you ask your wife to fix something else?"

"Oh, I'm not married," was the reply. "I make my own lunch."

I make my own lunch too—and I make my own life. If anywhere in my life I still think that someone else or something else is the cause of anything, I'm abdicating the very gift that makes me human, the divine quality that makes us most like the divine, my freedom.

When I speak of freedom as a divine quality, I mean the gift of free will. Free will is a basic right bestowed upon us by our creator so that we can learn to be cocreators. We don't ever create anything. We don't create out of nothing. Only source/God creates out of nothing; but it is in co-creation with source/God that everything comes into being. Because we have this right we should use it; we should take advantage of the precious gift that it is.

If you had purchased or was given a ticket to a buffet, you would then have the *right* to take from this buffet whatever you would choose to take. You paid for the ticket—or someone bought it for you—and that gave you the *right* to eat whatever you *choose*. Would you sit down and complain that you didn't get any dessert, or salad, or something that you didn't choose? Not if you are thinking at all. You would get up and go get it.

We often complain because things aren't the way we want them to be. We've already been given the whole gift—to make the choices that we make—and then we say, "It's not happening. It must be something else out there."

Barbara Marx Hubbard, futurist, author, and dear friend and mentor of mine, rewrote a line from the US *Declaration of Independence.* She enlarges Thomas Jefferson's great statement to say, "We hold these truths to be self-evident. All people are born creative, endowed by our Creator with the inalienable right to realize our creativity, for the good of ourselves and the world."[1]

That is true freedom. So freedom, as a divine quality, is about our ability to make choices and be all we are and all we can become.

When it's put that way, who doesn't want freedom? Why, then, are we not living in total freedom all the time? In fact, most of us reject the gift of freedom, because along with it comes responsibility.

Freedom does not mean the right to do whatever one wants. Freedom is not license. Freedom also doesn't mean free from consequences. That's what most people don't like about the law of cause and effect. Often, rather than accept responsibility for our consequences, we claim not to be free. Most of us say, "I didn't have a choice." How many times do you hear yourself say that?

Who chooses your life? Who chooses the things that happen to you? Is it someone else out there? I once heard Stephen Covey at a seminar tell a story about a student coming to him and saying, "I'm in this tennis final and I have to miss the last class. Stephen Covey said, "You *have* to?" And the student said, "Yes, I have no choice. I'm in these finals." Covey worked with him until this young boy could say, "I'm choosing to go to these finals instead of coming to class." When he said that, Covey said, "Of course, go to the finals."

"I have no choice." How often we give up our freedom by saying these words.

The only way to be truly free is to thoroughly accept responsibility. The idea of real freedom is sometimes a pretty scary proposition for most of us. We choose not to be free whenever we don't choose responsibility for what happens in our lives. When we don't choose responsibility, we are choosing to play the victim. I do that without realizing it most of the time. This is an either-or mentality. *"Either* somebody else is at fault, *or* somebody else is at cause. Therefore, I am not responsible. I must be the poor victim."

In small ways, I still find that I go into victim mode daily. There's always something out there that is the cause of what I am doing. A lot of times I don't realize it, certainly not intentionally, but I often become unconscious of the feelings and beliefs that are directing my actions. Notice how often you say something is *because*. That's another way of saying, "I'm not responsible." We go unconscious because we do not want the responsibility of our choices, so at least we can then say, "Well, I was unconscious. That was the problem." We get really subtle with this excuse.

I am not free whenever I believe in cause and effect at all, when I think something else causes what happens in my life; in fact, when I think that anything has a cause at all. Often, when you find yourself looking for the cause of what is happening, check to see that it isn't just another way of deflecting responsibility.

I once heard someone say that anything you say after the word *because* is actually a cop-out from taking responsibility. I used to teach critical thinking, and this is one of the logical fallacies that we are all guilty of: thinking that something that comes after something else is actually caused by it. We do it all the time. This happened after this, so we say the second thing must have been caused by the first thing.

Here's an illustration: One of my dear friends was recently given a new medication by her doctor. Right after she started to take it, she took a trip to Mexico and wound up getting Montezuma's revenge. When her doctor questioned her if she had done anything different on this trip to Mexico, she realized that she had drunk some fruit juice—and of course, the fruit had been washed off by the water in Mexico—and many of us who have traveled there, know not to drink the water. What caused the problem here? The water, the fruit juice, the medication? We'll never really know. (She told me later that the real cause was probably that she didn't have enough tequila while she was there, because that would kill or cure anything!)

We want to know causes, so we can put the incident behind us and not have to take responsibility for it

When you get sick, do you decide it was *because* you were in an airplane, or a crowded room, or a child sneezed near you? Now, if you did a survey of everyone else who was in that plane, or in that crowded room, or who had ever been sneezed on by a sick child, I guarantee you would discover that most of the others did not get sick—probably at least 90 percent. So, how did any of those things become the cause? If they were the cause, wouldn't they be the cause in all cases?

We think something has to be the cause of everything that happens in our lives. We are so wired to be right that we've got to be certain that something is causing things, so we can dismiss what happens and let it go. When we do this, we give up our freedom. And we wonder why we don't feel free in life.

The only way to experience freedom is to give up the word *because* and to *be cause*. We act in the image and likeness of God/source, and to be source is to cause everything. Source or God is the cause of all things, the creator of all things. If I am acting in the image and likeness of God, then I, too, need to be cause of everything in my life.

I don't think the Creative Source ever said, "That happened by accident." "I caused the planets and the moon and the stars, but those humans? I had nothing to do with that." I bet there are times it would love to say that!

Think about this. That's what we want to say. "I'm the cause of these things. I like when I cause *this* in my life, but I really don't cause *those* things."

Whenever something doesn't go as expected, we tend to "blame" someone else for what went wrong. In doing so, we lose a tremendous learning opportunity.

The world makes progress by learning from mistakes. I wish it weren't so, but that seems to be one of the ways we learn. When we blame someone else, it gives that person power over us and over the situation. For example, have you ever said something like, "If Helen had done what she agreed she would do, then this would never have happened." That may be true. However, this statement gives Helen the total power over the situation.

Being responsible doesn't mean blaming yourself or anyone else. Being responsible is recognizing that life is a mirror and that it reflects back to us. "If my mother hadn't done that when I was three...." "If so and so hadn't done ... when I was twelve." "If I hadn't been rejected when I was...." You fill in the blanks. When we blame the other person, we are not responsible. We are out of control. But when you are out of control, you have no freedom. So, once again, you are saying, "I'm not accepting this quality of freedom." Remember, however, that not blaming means not blaming *ourselves* either. In accepting true responsibility we bring about a sense of relief, rather than guilt.

Some people have learned not to blame others—at least most of the time. But at other times we tend to subtly justify what happened, which is really another way of blaming. For example, you might say, "I would have gotten here on time, but there was a lot of traffic." I love it when I start class, and three-fourths of the class makes it on time, but the rest come in late and say, "There was a lot of traffic." You know what? We all came through the same traffic.

I know that when I'm late because I got caught up in traffic, it simply means that I didn't allow enough time for anything to happen other than zipping through green lights all along the way. I left myself no time. That's the truth—not that there was a lot of traffic.

Or you might say, "I would have gotten what I promised done except that I had traveled all night yesterday and I was too tired to focus on it today." This is just another form of blame. Instead of blaming a person, however, we blame the circumstances.

My favorite excuse is, "I was late because I got a phone call." Are we obliged to answer the phone when it rings? When the phone came into existence, we gave up our freedom. Then we curse the people calling us, especially telemarketers, because they shouldn't be calling. The truth is, we don't need to immediately answer every call.

I'm using some simple examples to show how often in our lives we make up the story that something else is in charge. Instead of blaming the circumstances, we'll use any old excuse. No matter how reasonable the justification, we are shirking responsibility when we do this and thereby losing our freedom.

Some people do a lot of blaming and justifying because they are "more advanced." We are masters at beating ourselves up: "I did the dumbest thing!" Do you really want to be calling yourself that? "Oh, I didn't mean it." We don't even want to take responsibility for the words we say. I can't tell you how many people say things, and when I respond, "Did you hear what you are saying?" They reply, "I didn't say that," or, "I didn't mean that." *Then don't say it.*

Why do we say the things we say and don't even want to take responsibility for it? We want the words to roll off our lips and hopefully the universe won't hear us, because we didn't really mean it. Our unconscious or subconscious mind is continually speaking through our lips. That's why I'm in a spiritual community, so people can remind me. Are we really free if we aren't saying what we mean? How free are we if we say things as a kind of knee-jerk reaction? We've lost our freedom here too.

When will we allow ourselves to recognize the part we play in *everything* that happens? We are co-creators. It is only by accepting responsibility that we actually have optimal control, direction, and command over our lives.

Please underline an important distinction here: responsibility is not the same as blame. The fact that I didn't take time to get somewhere on time doesn't mean there is anything wrong with me. But that's where our minds go. "There must be something wrong with me if I'm doing this." Well, maybe if you're doing something continually—say, you are constantly late and people are constantly being disrupted by your late arrival—you may want to look at that as a nonproductive way of living. But there is nothing wrong with you. It doesn't make you a bad person. We don't want to take responsibility because if it is someone else's fault, than we don't have to be bad. We blame ourselves. But that's not what responsibility means.

Responsibility is the ability to respond. It is also recognizing that we are cause in every experience of our lives. We've been given the gift of freedom to be used at every moment of our lives.

Life is a succession of choices. I frequently look at crowds of people and wonder which choice made them who they are. Have you ever looked at what choice made you who you are? When you are driving a boat and you go off by one degree, do you think you'll ever make your destination? You were heading one place and went off by one degree. Think about where you'd be in an hour—or ten years. Nowhere near where you started out. Every choice of even one degree is important in our life.

In the movie, *Harry Potter and the Chamber of Secrets*, a teacher tells Harry, "It isn't your talents that make you who you are, it's your choices."[2] Why am I not a concert pianist today? I have a lot of talent. I played the piano when I was a young child. It was challenging for my parents to buy it, and even more challenging for me to practice. So, why am I not a concert pianist today? Because I didn't choose to practice along the way.

Do you think you become things only because you're born that way? "It's God's fault that I'm not a concert pianist, because God didn't give me that ability." That's how we think. "I didn't have that ability. I wasn't born with a silver spoon in my mouth. I didn't have the advantages somebody else had." I can spend my whole life saying, "Therefore I can't have anything." That's what we tend to do. We constantly blame the past, but in one way we are blaming source. "I didn't get the talent." "I was not born a blonde." (You can make a choice about that!)

I repeat: we are inherently free. Freedom is a divine quality that we inherit, but much of the time, we don't really want freedom.

We have to choose to live in freedom. Besides not wanting to accept responsibility, another reason we don't really want freedom is that to be truly free, we must pay the price of discipline. That's why I didn't practice the piano. I chose to be out with my friends, or to read a good book, or do something else. There's a price to pay if you want to make certain choices. We often say, "I just can't do it," for whatever reason. But what we are really saying is, "I don't want the discipline. I don't want to have to do that in my life."

Most people would rather be told what to do than to use their personal freedom to make up their minds about what they really want. It is much easier to be told what to do.

This is also true when we pray. We make statements based on what we know is the truth, and many of us would rather pray to a God out there, asking someone else out there to do something for us. If I'm really honest with myself, I would much rather pray that way. "Would somebody please fix this situation? I don't want to be responsible for it. I got myself into this mess, but please, somebody help me out of it." That's what we attempt to do most of the time. We'd really like someone else to tell us what to do. Your first reaction to this might be, "Not me!—I don't want to be told what to do."

I invite you to look deeper.

Is there anywhere in your life where are you not living fully? Is there anywhere in your life where you have made a compromise to be less than you know you could be? Perhaps it's in a job. You stay because the benefits are too good to give up, even though you'd rather be doing almost anything else.

After I left the convent and started to work for a major telecommunications company, back when it was a conglomerate, my co-workers and I used to call our benefits package the "golden handcuffs." I was the only one in our cohort who had a master's degree, and I was making $16,000 a year. I remember being so proud of that, because everyone else was making $10,000–$12,000. I hated the job. I was a programmer behind a cubicle. (It's hard for people who know me now to imagine that.)

Whenever I finished my work too soon, my boss would admonish me to "look busy." I hated it, but I stayed there many more years than I would like to admit because it was very convenient. I have a friend who stayed there to this day, who still doesn't love what he is doing; but the pay is too good and he has too many benefits. He chose security and spent his life doing something he hated.

We don't like to take the time to figure out what we'd rather be doing. We get comfortable being "unfree." It's much more comfortable to stay where we are and be uncomfortable than it is to be uncomfortable about change.

Or we stay in a relationship when there's little or no love there, because it's easier to stay in something that's known than to face the unknown. I once heard someone say that the marriage vows say, "Till death do us part," and we assume that means physical death. But many people have been in relationships where "death" was present. We are told that death means being apart physically, but that's not always the case. However, it's easier to stay with something that we know rather than face the unknown. We don't really want to choose freedom, because freedom can be challenging.

Another example is religion. Have you stayed in your religion longer than you really felt comfortable? Or have stayed in a friendship when you knew it was over? You keep the friendship going even though there is nothing left there. You feel this obligation. Where is your freedom?

Anytime you don't choose and you let life default, you are not living in freedom. Anytime you don't live the idea that consciousness is everything, you are really saying, "I'd rather not be free. I don't want the responsibility to change my consciousness."

By the way we live our lives, we sometimes say, "I'd still rather think that there is someone or something outside me that causes things to happen, whether I accept that it is a benevolent God or decide that it is some other power. Maybe not an evil force, but a person or even a superstitious belief that I give that power to. It's easier than changing my consciousness."

That telecommunications company was a power in my life. It wasn't source energy running my life at that time, because freedom is an attribute of the divine. If I choose to be stuck somewhere, then the divine is not running my life. This is not an easy teaching. It's easier to believe that if you pray to God out there, you may get what you want, or you may not, depending on God's whim. But eventually, you'll have it in the hereafter. That's an easier way to live—at least on the surface—than to say, "I am responsible for my consciousness and I can change my life by changing what I believe and what I think."

Thought I know this truth, I confess that, deep down, I still don't think that I have the power to change—at least in some areas of my life. I know that's not really true, but it feels that way sometimes. I'd rather give up my freedom than take the responsibility of deciding who I really am. If you find it scary to face your own magnificence, consider the wonderful passage from Marianne Williamson's *A Return to Love*.

Our deepest fear is not that we are inadequate.

Our deepest fear is that we are powerful beyond measure.

It is our Light, not our darkness, that most frightens us.

We ask ourselves, who am I to be brilliant, gorgeous, talented, fabulous?

Actually, who are you NOT to be?

You are a child of God. Your playing small

does not serve the World.

There is nothing enlightening about shrinking

so that other people won't feel unsure around you.

We were born to make manifest the glory of God that is within us.

It is not just in some of us;

it is in everyone.

As we let our own Light shine, we unconsciously give

other people permission to do the same.

As we are liberated from our own fear,

our presence automatically liberates others.[3]

I invite you to ponder those ideas. Ask yourself where in your life you are fearing freedom, and therefore blocking this divine quality that wants to come into your life in a greater way.

Choose today to accept the fact that you were born free and are meant to be free—free from the influence of others. Free of the thoughts and opinions of others. Free of your past. You are not living in the past, and you can be totally free from that. You are free to be the full expression of who we are, individually. Because we are individual expressions of the One Mind, One Power, One Life, this means you have self choice, volition, a conscious mind, complete freedom, and a power to back up that freedom.

In *The Science of Mind*, by Ernest Holmes, we read: "We cannot imagine a mechanical or unspontaneous individuality; to be real and free, individuality must be created in the image of Perfection and let alone to make the great discovery for itself."[4] That is the discovery of our freedom.

We are created with the possibility of limitless freedom and left alone to discover it ourselves. This discovery is called the awakening process.

Ultimate freedom is the freedom to be the divine self that you are, which includes living as a fully balanced and conscious being. When you remember that you are liberated, you are spontaneous in your expression of life, and you express in ways that are in harmony with the greatest good for everyone concerned.

I watched a video last night of people laughing, just people laughing. They looked so silly. Most of us don't want to look like that. We're worried that people might think there is something strange about us, so we hold ourselves back from laughing.

How many things do you hold yourself back from? When you accept your freedom, you are at ease wherever you find yourself. You have the freedom to just be you. When you are free, you don't have to worry about what the other person is thinking, feeling, being, or doing. When you are really free, you can totally allow another person to be free, because you don't depend on their being anything. And that's even your partner, or anyone else in your life. Your freedom doesn't depend on what he does or says. Nothing binds you. You are a true individual, unique and expressive. Life takes on more joy when you realize this.

No matter what quality you focus on, you get the rest of them. If you were totally free and allowed everyone else to be free, don't you think there would be more love in your life? There would be more joy in your life too. There would be so many more qualities in your life simply by focusing on freedom.

We have total freedom to choose at every moment, and we constantly experience the results of our thoughts and the results of our actions. What freedom that is! We think it's a burden, but in truth, it's amazing freedom to know that no one else has the power over your life but you.

If you don't like what's happening in your life, you have the power to change it. You don't have to wait until your mom or dad does something. You don't have to wait until your partner gets better; you don't have to wait until your children grow up; you don't have to wait for anything. You're the one who has the ultimate power and the ultimate freedom. Being free allows you to experience so much more of life.

The difference between freedom and bondage is simply the word *choice*. You have choice in every single moment, in every single experience. Choose to be conscious of your choice.

But, even that choice is yours.

Chapter 7

Joy

"I know that it is all good."

I'm writing this chapter during the Easter season, so I'd like to start this chapter by telling you my favorite Easter story—and it's true.

A minister was standing at the back of the church greeting people as they were leaving. "Good morning," she said to a little boy who was waiting in line to see her after church.

"I've been waiting to tell you something that happened to me," he said.

"Wonderful," she said.

"Ever since I was little, I always wanted to be a bunny rabbit. I always wished I were furry and free to hop and run all over. I wished and I wished but I finally gave up, because I saw that I was never going to get my wish and become a rabbit. Then, last week a miracle happened."

"Really," she chuckled, imagining that he had received a special pet rabbit.

"Yes," he said with his eyes wide in wonder. "After all this time of wishing, God gave me a dream one night, and in my dream I was a bunny rabbit and I felt what it was like to be furry and free and run and hop and play. I had a wonderful time and I got my wish."

"That's wonderful," she agreed.

"But that's not all," he said excitedly. "During my dream, God showed me how wonderful it is to be a bunny rabbit and when I woke up, I realized that the feelings that I wanted to feel in being a bunny rabbit are already inside me. So I've been carrying what I wanted with me all along."

His eyes were wide with recognition and hers were filled with tears of appreciation for his newly found inner splendor.

"Thank you for sharing your wonderful story with me," she managed to get out.

"I just thought you'd like to know," he said as he smiled and walked off with his mom into the crowd.

I'd also like to share two of my favorite joy quotes. The first is part of my personal covenant, and it's from the Jerusalem Bible version of the Old Testament, Zephaniah, 3:14–17: "Shout for joy, daughter of Zion, Israel shout aloud! Rejoice, exult with all your heart.... Yahweh your God is in your midst. He will exult with joy over you, He will renew you by his love; He will dance with shouts of joy for you; as on a day of festival."

Joy and happiness are not the same thing. I had some challenges this week, and that distinction became really clear to me. Happiness to most people is defined as the elation that accompanies good fortune. When things are going well, when the sun is shining, when we get a raise or a new job, when we think we are in love, when we get to hop like a bunny, we feel happy, and we confuse that with the quality of joy. Real joy is getting in touch with the stuff that's already inside us. Joy is the evidence of God's presence in the human experience. And divine energy/source/God/life force can never be absent! We have to learn to look for the evidence. It's there, sometimes in spite of what is happening in the outer world.

Have you ever cried and felt joy at the same time? I sure have. If so, then you know what I mean. Joy is the awareness that all is good. Even in the midst of struggle or suffering, God is here. This too is God. This too is good. We can never escape the presence of God. When we begin to see all of life as a perfect reflection of our thoughts, and we see that life always brings us what we send out, then we cannot help but rejoice in the perfection, because we notice that is exactly what is happening all the time. There's a great sense of relief and release in knowing this. We are really in charge. What we send out comes back.

The second of my favorite quotes (also attributed in various places on the Internet to Leon Bloy, French novelist and poet) is from Pierre Teilhard de Chardin, a Catholic priest and theologian: "Joy is the most infallible sign of the presence of God."[1] I've heard it paraphrased, "Joy is the echo of God's life in us." I like that quote and it leads me to tell you another story.

A man and his son were taking a walk in the forest. Suddenly his son trips and, feeling a sharp pain, screams, "Ahhhh!"

Surprised, he hears a voice coming from the mountain, "Ahhh!" Filled with curiosity, he screams, "Who are you?"

But the only answer he receives is, "Who are you?"

This makes him angry, so he screams, "You are a coward!" and the voice answers, "You are a coward!"

He looks at his father, asking, "Dad, what is going on?"

"Son," the man replies, "pay attention!" Then the father screams, "I admire you!"

The voice answers, "I admire you!"

The father shouts, "You are wonderful!"

And the voice answers, "You are wonderful!"

The boy is surprised, but still can't understand what is going on. Then the father explains, "People call this an 'echo,' but truly it is 'life'!"

—Author Unknown

_____

Life always gives you back what you give out. Life is a mirror of your actions and beliefs. If you want more love, give more love. If you want more kindness, give more kindness. If you want more understanding and respect, give more understanding and respect. This rule of nature applies to every aspect of our lives. Your life is not a coincidence, but a mirror of your own doings.

Joy is not something we get or obtain; joy is what we are. We can't search for joy; it is not outside of us. It is already right where we are. We have to let it reveal itself to us. Here's an important distinction to remember: joy is not a reactionary emotion; it is a causative energy. Let me repeat: joy is not a reactionary emotion; it is a causative energy. Joy doesn't just happen as a result of outer experience; we can release it from inside ourselves by active will.

Nisargadatta Maharaj (twentieth century Hindu sage) responded with this stunning answer to an inquiry about his not feeling sad in the face of circumstances that drive most people to despair, such as war and poverty: "In my world, nothing ever goes wrong."[2] He was saying that he lived in the world of spirit, and the rest is illusion. *A Course in Miracles* begins with the words, "Nothing real can be threatened. Nothing unreal exists. Herein lies the peace of God."[3]

We experience true joy then when we experience the presence of God. Everything I teach is about learning to live in this presence. It's all about living consciously. It's about living in awareness so that we stay in the present moment and not let ourselves be pushed by the past or pulled by the future. Living in the present is living in the presence.

I had a rather angry outburst directed at someone this week. I apologized to her and to those who witnessed it, because I was aware even as I was doing it that what I was experiencing at the moment was not what I was feeling anger over. Does this ever happen to you? Most of the time when we feel anger, it's not about what just happened. I wasn't totally conscious in the moment of the outburst, but I was immediately afterward. (The time lags are getting shorter—that's a sign of growth!)

Spiritual growth isn't about feeling good all the time, and it isn't about being perfect or about liking everything that happens in our lives. At the split second after the outburst, I could see the perfection in what was happening in me, as me, and through me. And in the pain I was feeling at the moment, and even with the tears I shed, I felt a deep sense of joy.

Does that sound strange to you? I was in touch both with the anger at the moment and where it was coming from, so I was in a state of being present and could feel the presence as a result. That's what I mean when I talk about consciousness. Many people think it means bliss. "I should feel wonderful all the time." But consciousness really is being conscious at the moment, so we don't get caught up in what is happening, and recognizing when places of healing are showing up in our lives.

Sometimes we think that if we are living the spiritual life, nothing should ever go wrong. We have this illusion that we're on a spiritual path, and so we wonder why these things happen. And, of course, why do they happen *to me*. We think we should never have a bad day. We reason, "I'm on a spiritual path. I've been praying for so long. So why do these things continue to happen?" As Americans, especially, we encounter a problem in the pursuit of happiness. That's sometimes what we are all about—the pursuit of happiness. It's easy to be blissful when we are in seclusion. It's easy to realize the presence of God when we are in meditation, and sometimes we even have moments of bliss. That's not what joy is about. Joy is the experience of the presence in every situation.

Joy is about continually living in divine grace. Living in divine grace means constantly living in a state of guidance. Notice that the word *dance* is at the end of the word *guidance*. Dancing is one of my favorite pastimes—and a great metaphor for living the spiritual life. Allowing life to flow from God's point of view, allowing ourselves to live in the presence, is a lot like dancing. When two people try to lead, nothing feels right. The movement doesn't flow with the music, and everything is uncomfortable and jerky. When one person realizes this and lets the other lead, both bodies begin to flow with the music. One gives gentle cues, perhaps with a nudge to the back, or by pressing lightly in one direction or another. It's as if two become one body, moving beautifully. The dance takes surrender, willingness, and attentiveness from one person, and gentle guidance and skill from the other. When you think of the word *guidance*, see *g* as God, followed by *u* and *i*. God, *u*, and *I*, dance! *God, you, and I dance.* Experiencing joy is about being in the dance with God.

Living in joy is trusting the guidance about your life at every single moment. There is nothing wrong, no matter what seems to be happening in your life. No matter what it looks like, this is the perfection

of life. Life follows exactly the impress of our thoughts. Are you willing to let God lead, as you do your part? *Let* means letting things be
just as they are and just as they are not. This is not an easy way. It
takes focus and discipline, commitment, and dedication to learn the
steps. I don't know about you, but there is a list of things in my life
that I want different. This "shouldn't be"—I want it *that* way. Isn't
that what causes us struggle? Isn't that what takes away our joy?
Whatever is, is. Whatever is not, is not. Let us allow ourselves to stop
fighting life, because it is only in accepting *what is* that any transformation takes place.

Ernest Holmes, the founder of Religious Science, defines joy as
"the emotion excited by the expectancy of good."[4] This is not feeling
that I want things to be different because they are not good now, but
expecting good at all times. So what is right now is good, and I can't
see it any other way. When you know the presence of God in all
things, you have to expect the good. I firmly believe that we are here
to experience joy. Scripture tells us that "it is the Father's good pleasure to give us the kingdom" (Luke 12:32). So no matter what is taking place in your life right now, no matter how else you would like it
to look, joy will only be realized when you get to say, "This is it. Right
here, right now is where the presence of God is. God is—not will be
when—but in the here and now, God is."

Author Leo Buscaglia used to teach seminars on love. At one such
seminar, he told this story about his mother and their "misery din-

ner." It was the night after his father had come home and said it looked as if he would have to go into bankruptcy because his partner had absconded with their firm's funds. His mother went out and sold some jewelry to buy food for a sumptuous feast. Other members of the family scolded her for it. But she told them, "The time for joy is now, when we need it most, not next week." Her courageous act rallied the family.[5]

We have an opportunity to live in joy every single day. Don't postpone happiness until the debts are settled and relationships rearranged. Joy doesn't exist out in the world somewhere; we find it inside. Joy doesn't depend on what's happening *to* us, but what we are allowing *in* us. Like all things joy is a matter of choice. When we "lighten up," we "enlighten up" the world.

Taking ourselves too seriously is the opposite of joy. We make up meanings for everything. I do this. "This must mean—" and of course, it's the wrong meaning. "I don't have this, therefore—." "This is not in my life, therefore—." "I don't have the money I want. I don't have the relationship I want. I don't have the body I want. I don't have the health I want." You name it. "And therefore, things must be—"

We lose our joy when we think things should be another way than what they are, and when we want to control the situation and make it into something it is not. So right now I invite us to quit complaining about anything. Are you willing to take that on today, even about the little things? Think for a moment about your constant complaint, the one nagging at you, whatever it is. Are you willing to let that go? What a joyful experience that could be if we just let that one complaint go. You don't have to let them all go at once. Just the one—the big one that you carry!

If we get that we are the joy we are seeking, and really begin to live more in the presence, then we will start to realize that we have nothing to complain about. I invite you to look at ways you can bring joy wherever you are.

We're told that angels have wings because they take themselves lightly. Notice this week when you are making a drama out of something, and see what story you are telling yourself. "What am I telling myself about what's happening? What's really happening, and what's my story about what's happening?" Look to see the facts of what is happening. Facts are things you can put in a wheelbarrow, not what you think you are seeing in a situation.

If you are saying something like, "When he did this, it made me …" or, "She said this, and it must have meant …," then stop and say, "Would someone who was observing what happened be able to say that's what happened?" What would a newspaper photo show of what actually happened?" If someone frowns, for example, we say, "Obviously he is angry or obviously…." What would the picture look like if it were a static picture? We don't just see what is happening; we make up what it means. And that's when we lose our joy. What we make up makes us lose our joy. Trust me—I know. I'm good at it.

Train yourself to be a joy detective. Look for the joy, instead of looking for what's wrong. Do you look for what's wrong with the picture, whether it's a situation outside yourself or something in you? When you are tempted to complain about something, try complimenting yourself instead. Complain. Stop. Switch to a compliment.

And if there are experiences that you don't feel joyful about, ask yourself, "What's good about this situation?" When you ask yourself, "What's wrong with me?" your brain will give you an entire list of what's wrong or why something isn't working. Your brain will tell you it's because your mother did this when you were three and this happened when you were seven. That happens, doesn't it? The questions we ask ourselves are really important. So the question we must ask is, "What's good about this situation?" Get back to the original joy. Then find at least ten things a day you can compliment—and say them out loud to someone else. It's a great way to experience joy. You can't help but be joyful if you are spending the day thinking of what to compliment. Think about that, and begin to look at what's working in your life and in the lives of others.

We have learned over and over in life that supply is not in getting but in giving. If you want more joy in your life, ask yourself, "Where am I sharing and where am I serving?" When you share your talent, it delights others. If you want joy, get your eyes off yourself and get them first on God. Then open your eyes to those around you and see what they might need. If you want joy in your life, find a need and fill it; find a wound and heal it. When you do, you will discover that joy finds you; you don't find joy.

The Prayer, found in many forms and attributed to Saint Francis of Assisi, reminds us of this:

> Lord, make me an instrument of thy peace.
>
> Where there is hatred, let me sow love.
>
> Where there is injury, pardon.
>
> Where there is doubt, faith.
>
> Where there is despair, hope.
>
> Where there is darkness, light.
>
> Where there is sadness, joy.
>
> O, Divine Master, grant that I may not so much seek
>
> to be consoled as to console;
>
> to be understood as to understand;
>
> to be loved as to love.
>
> For it is in giving that we receive;
>
> it is in pardoning that we are pardoned;
>
> it is in dying to self that we are born to eternal life.

Jesus, the master teacher, told his followers in his final words, "I have told you this so that my joy may be in you and that your joy may be complete" (John 15:11). He did not say that we would always be "happy," but he did promise joy. Happiness is concerned with what "happens to us," but joy is connected to what is "going on within us." Happiness comes and goes, but joy is a constant, because it is one of our inherited qualities.

Choose now to live in that quality. Say yes to whatever it is that life is holding out for you at this moment. Look within. Be still—and know—in the words of the famous "Prayer for Protection" by James Dillet Freeman, Unity teacher and poet often said at the end of a Unity Sunday service.

The light of God surrounds us,
The love of God enfolds us,
The power of God protects us,
The presence of God watches over us,
Wherever we are, God is. And all is well.

Chapter 8
Love

"The divine in me sees and greets the divine in you."

Ah, love. It's almost everybody's favorite word and the quality that is most identified with God. We've heard for years that God is love, and if we inherit the divine qualities, then who we are in essence is love. What does that mean, and do we know what love is? I won't presume to define it for you in one chapter, but we'll begin to take a look.

At our core, we question the meaning of words such as *loving*, *loved*, and *loveable*. We ask ourselves, "Will they love me if they find out who I really am?" "Will I still be loveable to so and so after I do this?" "Was what I just said really loving?" We all live with the question of what love is, and we could spend our whole lives exploring the answer.

Part of our confusion about love comes from our being limited to only one English word (*love*) with many shades of meaning. For example, you may love your partner, love your job, or love drinking wine and eating chocolate. When we say that love is a divine quality, what do we mean?

The ancient Greeks had a clearer understanding of love. Like the Eskimos, who have multiple words for the word *snow*, they used at least four different words to describe love. The one that we hear most about and usually equate with love itself is *eros*. When we talk about *eros*, we are talking about sexual passion, arousal, its gratification and fulfillment. The origin of the word came from the mythical god Eros, the god of love. Many popular songs talk about this kind of love. This is the kind of love we "fall into," not the love we already are; because if you can "fall in," then you can "fall out." In real love you want the other person's good. In romantic love, you want the other person.

People constantly search in vain for fulfillment through human love. They go from one romance to another in search of true love. There is a longing in us for love, which tells us that there must be something that meets that longing. No human love can meet the needs of the human soul. Instead, it's the love of God that can fill the void in the human heart, because that's who we are. It's ourselves searching for our selves. The divine quality that we know as love must be more than this experience that our society speaks of.

We often think that love is *storge*, the Greek word for the familial bond of love that knits together family members with each other. This is the kind of love we talk about when we say, "Blood is thicker than water." Many people spend much of their adult lives trying to find this kind of love if they feel it was missing in their adolescence. Long after parents are gone, many adults still attempt to please them, still trying to get their love. How many things do we do in order to please our parents, even when they are no longer with us? We look for and create substitute families when our own are dysfunctional or not the people we want to associate with any longer.

We long for family. Those who did not experience this kind of love as children tend to search for it for the rest of their lives. (Therapists can tell us better how many people are looking for this kind of love.) Witness how many people get married young to create the kind of family they always longed for. It's even popular today to create "families of choice." When people haven't reconciled with their family of origin, they look somewhere else for it. It is part of our nature to experience *storge*, and we do whatever it takes to find it. We mourn it when it isn't there. This confirms that there is a longing in us for family. It tells me again that there is a longing in us for something here.

Then there is *phileo*, the kind of love that comes from a loving friendship based upon common interests. It can involve a shared interest or shared commitment to a common cause, or cherished ideals we share in common. This love is often accompanied by and based on warm feelings and affection. But it's not lasting; when those feelings are gone, we often claim that love is gone as well. How many friends did you have when you did that peace march in the 1960s, for instance? Those were your "best friends ever." Who do you still know who was at your wedding? We constantly search for love, but it seems like it ends or we can lose it. So this must not be what the divine quality of love means. If love is a quality that we are, it can't end. It's not something you can have today and be gone tomorrow. What, then, is it?

God's love—the divine quality that I am writing of—includes all the above forms of love, but goes far beyond it. It is sometimes thought of as *agape*. This love seeks the highest good for the other. Unlike *eros*, which is based primarily on physical chemistry, or *storge*, which is also based on biology and connection, or even *phileo*, which is the natural inclination, based upon feelings and affection, *agape* is a decision-based love—coming from the will, not feeling.

Romantic love is something relatively new in our culture. Years ago, people didn't marry because they loved one another the way we talk about it today. Marriages were arranged. I remember asking my grandmother, whose marriage was arranged, "Did you love Grandpa?" "I learned to, I chose to," she said. He was brought here to marry her. One of the women who used to do my nails also has a pre-arranged marriage. Her Vietnamese parents brought her husband over to marry and take care of her. Arranged marriages still happen today. These people have learned to make love a decision, something that

comes from the will. It seeks the betterment of others, even its enemies, regardless of feelings. When you learn to love without necessarily having the feeling, you learn to love more broadly. That kind of
love doesn't seem to come naturally to me.

So what is this quality of which we speak, since these qualities are
our inherent nature? *Eros, storge, philio,* and *agape* are forms of
love—and they are all a part of what we are speaking of here. But the
essence of the quality of which we speak is something deeper. It
comes from the Aramaic word *rakma,* a universal love that declares, "I
love you because it is my nature to love." You do not have to change
for me to practice unconditional love and goodwill in both thought
and action." Stephen R. Covey, the author of *Seven Habits of Highly
Successful People,* said, "Love, the feeling, is the fruit of love, the
verb."[1] Think about that. The fruit of the action we take because of
our nature is what creates love; it's the decision to love, not waiting
for it to happen. That's what most of us do; we wait for love to come,
rather than know that love is who we already are.

When it sees something unlike itself, unconditional love looks past
it. It can go beyond, because love that is God always seeks the highest
good. This is the kind of love that seeks the best out of each person.
Universal love doesn't look at whether or not someone is worthy to be
loved. We all make these judgments. "Should I love this person or
not? Does he measure up? Is he really up to my standards here?" Why
do we do this?" The love of God says, "I don't care what you do. I

don't care who you are. I will love you. I will seek the best for you. I will seek the good things for you. I will seek to do the good things for your life. I will lift you up and will bless your life. I will make you a better person than you are. I want to make you better than you are."

Isn't that what life does? Doesn't life constantly call us to be more than we already are? No matter what's happening in our lives, love is a constant call that says, "I want more for you. I want to give you all I have. I want you to have the good." This love seeks the good of another person and doesn't count whether he deserves it. There's nothing you can do to deserve love. Isn't that good news? How many of us strive continually in order to deserve love? We think we have to do something or at least be something or someone in order to be loved.

A story from Africa beautifully illustrates this kind of love. When a woman in a certain African tribe knows she is pregnant, she goes out into the wilderness with a few friends, and together they pray and meditate until they hear the song of the unborn child. They recognize that every soul that comes into this world has its own vibration that expresses its uniqueness and purpose. When the women attune to the song, they sing it out loud. Then they return to the tribe and teach it to everyone else.

When the child is born, the community gathers and sings the child's song to him or her. Later, when the child enters education, the village gathers and chants the child's song. When the child passes through the initiation to adulthood, the people again come together and sing. At the time of marriage, the person hears his or her song. Finally, when the soul is about to pass from this world, the family and friends gather at the person's bed, just as they did at his or her birth, and they sing the person to the next life.

In this African tribe there is one other occasion upon which the villagers sing to the child. If at any time during his or her life the person commits a crime or an aberrant social act, the individual is called to the center of the village and the people in the community form a circle around this person. Then they sing their song to him.

The tribe recognizes that the correction for antisocial behavior is not punishment; it is love and the remembrance of identity. When you recognize your own song, you have no desire or need to do anything that would hurt another. That's tapping into the quality of love that we are.

You experience this kind of universal love when someone knows your song and sings it to you when you have forgotten it. Those who love you are not fooled by mistakes you make or dark images you hold about yourself. They remember your beauty when you feel ugly; your wholeness when you are broken; your innocence when you feel guilty; and your purpose when you are confused.

You may not have grown up in an African tribe that sings your song to you at crucial life transitions; but life itself always reminds you when you are in tune with yourself and when you are not. When you feel good, what you are doing matches your song, and when you feel awful, it doesn't. It comes to us naturally. Our feelings are a great barometer. They are the ways that life or God or good within us remind us of who we really are. That's the quality I am speaking of when I talk about love. This quality is our nature, but often we forget. However, we can remember who we are as we practice. We can practice unconditional love one person at a time.

Who can you remind of his or her true self this coming week—or, better still, today? Is there someone in your life who might need that reminder? What will you say? What will you do? It's worth thinking about. We can unleash this quality in us by practicing, being the "godlings" we are, who give up on no one. Who have you given up on? Is there someone in your past whom you've written off? You might say, "Never that person. No way will I reconcile with him or her." Who is that someone that you can call upon today in a whole new way?

God loves us not because we are loveable, but we become loveable because God loves us. We can do the same thing for one another. Have you ever noticed how someone else seems to change when you begin to accept him as he is and not try to change him? People don't change because we want them to change; people change when we love them enough that they are willing to change. Love is not about control. It's an allowing. Unconditional love says of every single one of us, "I love you. You are precious and special to me. I love you as if you were the only human being on earth. I love you and there is nothing you can do to make me love you more, because I already love you perfectly. Stop trying to make yourself loveable. Stop trying to do the things you think I need to love you."

When we begin to see each other this way, we are saying *Namaste*, a Sanskrit word that loosely translated means, "The divine in me sees and loves the divine in you. I see your essence, and immediately I look beyond appearances and cannot help but love you." When we see the good in each other, that love just comes forth. When I look at you, I see myself loving myself, God loving itself. That's what comes naturally.

Victor Hugo in *Les Miserables* said, "To love another person is to see the face of God." [2] Love is what every spiritual teacher tells us we are here for. What's the purpose of life? The master teacher, Jesus, said it simply, "Love one another, as I have loved you" (John 13:34). "As the Father has loved me, so have I loved you" (John 15:9). He reminds us that we can have that same love for one another.

The *Course in Miracles* repeats this: "Teach only love, for that is what you are."[3] In his book, *The Divine Milieu*, Pierre Teilhard De Chardin writes, "The day will come when, after harnessing space, the winds, the tides, and gravitation, we shall harness for God the energies of love. And on that day, for the second time in the history of the world, we shall have discovered fire."[4]

In preparation for becoming a minister years ago, I was asked to write my eulogy. I wrote, "We are each gathered here today to celebrate the life of Toni LaMotta, because we all felt loved in her presence." When life is over, it's never about how many toys you have accumulated, but about how much you have loved.

Many people are looking for love, or bemoaning the fact that we don't have enough love. Notice what you are focusing on. Are you asking, "How can I get more?" The real question is, "How can I express more of the love that I already am?"

There's a classic story told about Gandhi that expresses this type of unconditional loving.

> As Gandhi stepped aboard a train one day, one of his shoes slipped off and landed on the track below him. He was unable to retrieve it, as the train was moving. To the amazement of his companions, Gandhi calmly took off his other shoe and threw it back along the track to land close to the first. Asked by a fellow passenger why he did so, Gandhi smiled. "The poor man who finds the shoe lying on the track," he replied, "will now have a pair that he can use."[5]

I invite you to look at your own life and ask, "How can I express more of the love that I already am?" not, "How can I get more love?" Remember the story about the child hugging a teddy bear? We can hug stuffed animals or we can remember why Jesus came: to teach us to love one another as he loved us.

We can love unconditionally. Actually, unconditional love is the most natural love. The other stuff we've added over the years. It's not unnatural, just forgotten. It's natural because it is what we are made of, the substance of the universe. God is love. Love isn't a sometimes thing. It is a divine activity, a cosmic force, and a spiritual gift. As we make ourselves receptive to the idea of love, we become lovable. It's not what we do—it's what we allow. To the degree that we embody love, we are love. Did you ever notice that people who love a lot are loved a lot? It's never the other way around.

We are nothing without love. We often confuse that to mean that we need to have an object of our love to be someone or something. So many songs, in essence, say, "You're nobody 'til somebody loves you," or, "I'll be fine when I find love." Love can be felt for another, but love is not primarily a relationship to a specific person. It does not need an object on which to focus. Instead, it's like a powerful floodlight that brightens an entire room, rather than a flashlight that illuminates only where it is pointed. Love is an attitude that determines how we relate to the world. If we love one person and are indifferent to the rest, we are like the flashlight. This is not love, but a dependent attachment to something that makes us temporarily feel good. We can lose it, because if that person goes away, or changes, or dies, we think we don't have love anymore. How many people say, "I lost the love of my life"? You can't lose love. It is who you are. Yet many people believe that love begins with an object to love, rather than it being an indwelling faculty to be lived.

If we don't see love as an activity of our spirit, probably the best-known divine quality, then we can easily believe that all that is necessary to express love is to find the right object. This attitude is like the person who wants to learn to paint, but won't take art lessons, claiming that when the right scene is found, he or she will paint it perfectly. That's absurd. The fact is that we don't need "the right person" in order to express love. When you truly love one person, any person, you are able to love all people. You love the world.

Be first what you want to attract. You can only receive on the outside what you are on the inside. You already are the love that you are seeking. Do not look for love; release the love you are and it will find you. You attract yourself—always.

A group of women were at a Bible study. They were studying the Malachi 3 from the Old Testament. The Lord Almighty is speaking and he tells of sending a messenger who will prepare the way before him (v. 1). God describes the messenger by saying, "He will sit as a refiner and purifier of silver" (v. 3). The verse puzzled the women. They wondered what this statement meant about the character and nature of this messenger. One of the women said, "I'll go find out the process of refining silver, and I'll get back to the group at the next Bible study." And that week, the woman called a silversmith and

made an appointment to watch him at work. She didn't mention anything about the reason she wanted to know, beyond her curiosity
about the process of refining silver.

As she watched the silversmith, he held a piece of silver over the
fire and let it heat up. He explained that in refining silver, one needed
to hold the silver in the middle of the fire where the flames were hot-
test to burn away all the impurities. The woman thought about God
holding us in a hot spot. She thought again about the verse that said
the messenger sits as a refiner and purifier of silver. She asked the silversmith if it was true that he had to sit there in front of the fire for
the whole time the silver was being refined. The man answered yes, he
not only had to sit there holding the silver, but he had to keep his eyes
on the silver the entire time it was in the fire. If the silver was left a
moment too long in the flames, it would be destroyed. The woman
went silent for a moment. Then she asked the silversmith, "How do
you know when the silver is fully refined?" He smiled at her and
answered, "That's easy. When I see my image in it."

When we become clear enough to see our own image as God sees
its image in us, then we see that image in one another. We find it only
when we start seeing it in ourselves. One of the best things you can do
to be healthy, happy, and master of your life is to love yourself unconditionally. Have you remembered to love yourself today? You might
want to put this reminder on your refrigerator or bathroom mirror:
"Have I loved myself today?"

To love and honor your inner self, and to treat yourself with respect and dignity, is the simplest way to experience peace and joy of living. What can you do to do that? The human mind is the only created thing that can consciously deprive itself of accepting God's love. Isn't that amazing? We think we're the higher level. My animals know how to accept love—in fact, they demand it. Humans reject love all the time. Erich Fromm said, "Our highest calling in life is precisely to take loving care of ourselves."[6] What if you gave up doing everything else but taking care of yourself? What would your life look like? I'm not talking about narcissism. What would true self-love look like?

When you change your attitude about yourself from negative to positive, everything else in your life will change for the better. One of the extraordinary secrets of this world is that life flows outward. It originates inside and is projected outward where it is perceived as the external world. We are not affected by other people or by situations and circumstances in the way we normally think we are. That's what we think happens. We believe that what is out there is creating what's going on in us. The truth is, we are affected by what happens inside us. We are affected by our own feelings, our own thoughts. Nothing outside us has any real power to affect us. So, we love ourselves by working on that inside. Eleanor Roosevelt once said, "No one can make you feel inferior without your consent."[7]

You were created to be completely loved and completely lovable for your whole life. It is amazing that we do not realize this, because underneath everything we think and feel, our essence or true nature is still intact. The reason we do not feel completely loved and completely lovable is that we do not fully identify with our spiritual nature. We identify with what is on the outside.

Do we really understand the nature and quality of God's love? When we think of love, we often think in terms of human love. That's why when we attempt to describe the love of God to others, we often fall far short.

There is a quality of love that is purer, deeper, and more profound than we humans can begin to grasp. It is the love that the world is dying for want of. This love is our very nature.

> In 1 Corinthians 13:4–8, we find the clearest definition of love: "Love is patient, love is kind. It does not envy, it does not boast, it is not proud. It is not rude, it is not self-seeking, it is not easily angered, it keeps no record of wrongs. Love does not delight in evil but rejoices with the truth. It always protects, always trusts, always hopes, always perseveres."

God is love, not will be when, but is now. And so are we.

Chapter 9
Order

"There is a time and a place for everything."

In the book of Ecclesiastes chapter 3 we read,

There is a time for everything,
and a season for every activity under heaven:

a time to be born and a time to die,
a time to plant and a time to uproot,

a time to kill and a time to heal,
a time to tear down and a time to build,

a time to weep and a time to laugh,

a time to mourn and a time to dance,

a time to scatter stones and a time to gather them,

a time to embrace and a time to refrain,

a time to search and a time to give up,

a time to keep and a time to throw away,

a time to tear and a time to mend,

a time to be silent and a time to speak,

a time to love and a time to hate,

a time for war and a time for peace.

One possible definition of the divine quality that we call order is in the statement: "There is a time and a place for everything." The word *order* usually means that there is a regular or harmonious arrangement, some kind of organization, a straightening out of things so as to eliminate confusion.

I remember as a child hearing that "order is heaven's first law." (I think my mother said that when she wanted me to clean my room.) My friend Judy used to say, "Order is about finding a place for everything and then it is about remembering where it is."

Order is really about knowing where everything is. That's the kind of order I hire an assistant for. This couldn't be what the divine quality is, or it would come naturally. Straightening out my desk does not come naturally to me! Keeping closets and drawers clean? For some it comes naturally, but for the rest of us …?

If you ever studied personality typing, (which teaches you the various ways that people do things like make decisions or take in information), then you understand there are many different ways of being. Some people are naturally neat and their dishes are always put away and all the socks are neatly placed by size and color. And others, well, it's somewhere in one of these piles. Good organization isn't what we mean when we say order is a divine quality. However, the fact that most of us, including myself, have a longing to have things in their proper place is an indication that we long for order.

Relax. I'm not going to tell you that order definitely means a clean desk, because then you'll check mine. Instead, living in order has a lot more to do with the way you view life.

What's important to you? What do you listen for? What are you hearing lately—when you listen to the news, when your friends talk, when you listen to your own internal dialogue?

What do your eyes see? Do you see a world that is torn by violence and terrorism? Do you see lack and limitation all around you? Do you see insufficiency? "not-enoughness"? Do you see random events happening with no control over them? Do you see chaos?

Or, do you see with a different set of eyes and hear with your inner ears that know without a doubt that *everything* is in perfect divine order? You first have to work with a different set of eyes. You have to work with a different set of ears, the ones that are really there. Most of us aren't living our lives as fully as we are capable of living. There's so much more beyond the surface. Like an iceberg, we see the tip and think that's what's there. We see the chaos. We see the things happening in the world, and we think that's so, and we live in that illusion.

I'd like to share a story that may shed some light on this idea.

A Navajo Indian and his friend were in downtown New York City, walking near Times Square in Manhattan. It was during the noon lunch hour and the streets were filled with people. Cars were honking their horns, taxicabs were squealing around corners, sirens were wailing. The sounds of the city were almost deafening.

Suddenly the Navajo said, "I hear a cricket."

His friend said, "What? You must be crazy. You couldn't possibly hear a cricket in all of this noise!"

"No, I'm sure of it," the Navajo said. "I heard a cricket."

"That's crazy," said the friend.

The Native American listened carefully for a moment, and then walked across the street to a big cement planter where some shrubs were growing. He looked into the bushes, beneath the branches, and sure enough, he located a small cricket. His friend was utterly amazed.

"That's incredible," said his friend. "You must have superhuman ears!"

"No," said the Navajo. "My ears are no different from yours. It all depends on what you're listening for."

"But that can't be!" said the friend. "I could never hear a cricket in this noise."

"Yes, it's true," came the reply. "It depends on what is really important to you. Here, let me show you."

He reached into his pocket, pulled out a few coins, and discreetly dropped them on the sidewalk. And then, with the noise of the crowded street still blaring in their ears, they noticed every head within twenty feet turn and look to see if the money that tinkled onto the pavement was theirs.

"See what I mean?" asked the Navajo. ""It all depends on what's important to you."

One wouldn't expect to hear crickets in the middle of New York City. Something is out of order. When we are experiencing the divine quality that is order, we start to become aware of perfection, the way things are when we are living in our true nature and being our true self. Do you know how we know there is order? Because when we feel like something is out of order, we don't feel good. We have this sense, this feeling, that something's not right. Something is out of order. You don't have to learn to do that; it's your natural state. If you can feel out of order, then this must mean there is a true order. Isn't that logical? I've given a lot of thought to this. I don't see that clearing up chaos is true order, but it feels good when it is cleared up. I don't see that when I'm doing things that aren't supporting my true nature that it is out of order, but I feel it is out of order. That means that there is something in me that knows what order is. I really do know and have an innate capacity to live in that order.

Things are also said to be in order when there is no clutter. I like to think that divine order is an uncluttered state of consciousness. That's my definition. It's knowing that there is a right place for everything, and that I know when things are not in their proper place, whether they are physical things, things in my life, or things in the universe.

The practice of feng shui uses compass directions and the magnetism of the earth to show that there is a certain order of things that puts balance into life. This ancient Eastern study tells us that there is a place for everything. The magnetic energy of the earth pulls certain things toward a particular way. Have you ever walked into a room and it didn't feel right? So you moved a plant from one corner to the other and then it felt right. Order is an instinct in all of us. You put a picture on the wall and know that something's not right. You move one thing and then it's right. What is this? That which knows within us, that which knows the order. Feng shui teaches us that it appeals to us to have balance and order.

Doesn't it make sense, then, to believe that if there is an order in the universe, there is also an order to the events in our lives? There is order in our physical body, and order in the universe, so how could things happen in our lives randomly? Do you think things just happen in life? Are you just a victim of circumstances? A belief in divine right order is knowing that everything that is happening in our life is happening because of what we need to experience in order to grow and change. There is a part of us—our true selves, our souls—that seems to know what it is we need in order to reach that ultimate goal of enlightenment. And so, somehow consciously or unconsciously—mostly unconsciously—that part of us orchestrates our life so that certain events happen to support that growth. And many of those events are not necessarily the hardships of life. (Is that what you thought?) They also include all the great stuff: "Look at how wonderful this is." "Look at how well this fell into place." "Look at the great things that I've had."

I'm not saying that life is preordained. Order is not about something happening that was known before. We know that life is all about choice. What I am talking about is that our soul, or our highest self, has and makes choices to bring every experience that we need into our life. Breathe with that. If you truly accept that, what will happen in your life? If you truly accept this, it can bring a great sense of relief. "I called this into my life. I called this here right now because it is the perfect experience for me to get to my next level, whatever it looks like." We don't define our experiences: "I like this experience, and I don't like that one. This is a good one, and this is not a good one." That's living two powers—this is God and this isn't. When I like it, it is God, and when I don't, well …

Nothing happens in our life that is not in divine order. Nothing! This is one to ponder. Do you believe that? The most important question we could ask ourselves that determines the entire events of our life is, "Do you believe that the universe is a friendly place?" That's an interesting way of saying, "Do you believe that everything is in perfect order?" It's the same question. Do I believe that the universe is going to randomly hand me some bad luck, that some things will happen that I don't want to happen because the universe is out to get me? Or do I believe that I live in a benevolent universe? Do I live under the protection and the absolute knowing that all is good? That all is God? Everything is perfect.

You may be thinking, "I don't know if I believe that." This is worth thinking about. It's innate in you to believe. Faith is not a gift that some people have and others don't. It's a gift we all have but we need to experience it by using it. It's not something you go out and get; it's something you just use.

Suppose you decide this week to believe this. What if, just this week only—unless you choose to go beyond that—you choose to believe that every single event, experience, person, conversation, and everything that happens is in the perfect divine order to happen? If you find things you don't like, guess who can change them, when you believe you can? If you believe that the universe is doing things *to* you, and you have no control and there is no order in the universe, then you might as well give up, because there's nothing you can do about it. But if you believe there is a perfect order and that your soul is experiencing and expressing exactly what you want, you will have a different experience.

The way you know that you really believe this is that you never complain. When we complain we're saying, "Something's wrong here; this shouldn't be happening. It shouldn't be happening to me; it shouldn't be happening this way. Life is unfair. The universe really is unfriendly, and there is no order out here." Is there something you are complaining about right now? I'm noticing that I complain about contractors, about what is happening around my house. I decided to let that go and see the order in the universe. But what if the situation never changes? We put a lot of energy into complaining. It's exhausting, and it comes from not believing there's a perfect order in the universe. It's believing that somebody else did something to us.

When we decide to focus instead on the divine quality of order, we say things just don't feel right. When they don't feel right, and then I remember there is a perfect order in the universe, I can stop and say at that moment, "This really is perfect, whatever this is." I have a friend whose husband used to say all the time, "This is it. And I am happy." Isn't that a great line? "This is it. And I am happy." So, you can't pay your bills? "This is it. And I am happy." So, you have a headache, or you get a diagnosis you don't like? "This is it. And I am happy." So, you lose your job, a friend walks out on you, or your love life ends? "This is it. And I am happy." Imagine living like that!

Back to those contractors I'm having problems with. People tell me that this is just the way contractors are here in Florida. But I have conversations with people who have problems with contractors all over the country. It's not just Florida. You can easily get agreement for anything you want to complain about. (That's part of how the Law of Attraction works.) Notice that like attracts like. When you hear yourself say, "See, it's true. All my friends say so," realize that of course your friends say so, because that's what you say and life is a mirror. We constantly bring agreement into our lives. If we don't believe things are in order, the people in our lives won't either. Maybe you need some new people in your life who can start believing these principles with you.

There is perfection in everything. Life will constantly hand us things to manage, things to experience, things to grapple with. When we accept the quality of order, it presents us with an opportunity to experience life as a series of opportunities to go beyond the senses, to go beyond the appearances, to go beyond what we are seeing and really recognize the truth behind everything. It's the opportunity to move beyond the little self that only sees the surface and live in the consciousness of our higher self—what Jung used to call our transpersonal self, that part of us that knows, and knows that it knows. That part of us that experiences good, and knows there is good. Even though on some days you feel it is quite small, it really is who you are. It is your essence.

Everything that happens in life is by divine setup. Our souls choreograph opportunities for us to wake up. We've chosen to have certain experiences. Everything has a reason; everything has a season. *"There's a time for every purpose under heaven."* There are never any accidents in our life—and that includes the little things as well as the big ones. It's all happening perfectly. Nothing happens randomly. There is a perfect order in the universe.

Do you think the divine organizer who created human bodies with twenty-seven feet of colon created an amazing body? If I were God I'd probably do it differently, but it's amazing how our bodies operate. Look at the ocean. It's amazing that it seldom overpowers the beach. There's perfection in the tides, the seasons, and the galaxies. Astronaut Edgar Mitchell, after being on the moon, talked about looking back down to this earth and seeing that it is only one little speck. This perspective sees the amazing order of this universe. It's enormous. Do you think the one who created that, the divine who can orchestrate and organize a world of galaxies, oceans, seas, and life spans, decided that when it came to humans, life would be random? That would be amazing. When we are aligned with order, that's when we grow. When we fight it, that's when life brings challenges and dramas and earthshaking events to call us back. That is what all those events are for. They are a wake-up call. They are saying, "Are you awake? Is this what you want to be living?"

When things happen in my life that shake me up I say, "Okay, listen. The universe is saying something. My soul is longing for something. What is it? Let's go in and look."

Do you know what is possible when we really understand (or embrace) knowing there is a perfect divine order? Many spiritual teachers stress that the most important spiritual practice is living in the now. Accepting order is accepting that at this moment you are right where you are doing exactly what you need to be doing with the perfect people you are meant to be with. (Look around you!) "This is it—and I am happy!" Can we say that in every circumstance? Can you do that on your job? At a town meeting? At a convention where half the group is thinking opposite from you? Can you do it in all circumstances, or in places where you say that "these are not my people"? Who are they then? Are they out of order? Or is everything happening perfectly?

Where do you long to be? Do you long to be somewhere else? If there is no order in your life, you think you should be someplace else.

In a different city, in a different home, in a different relationship, in a different job, perhaps. There's an old song that I'd like to give a different spin to: "When I'm not with the one I love, I love the one I'm with." I like thinking about that in terms of this message. What if we loved exactly where we were? The only way to find a new job, by the way, is to love the place you are at, and to give it everything you possibly have and be there perfectly. The only way to end a relationship is to love the relationship you are in. The only way to end anything you don't like is to love where it is and to know that it is perfect as it is. Keep breathing!

This is not about, "I need to be over there. Where I am stinks, and so I'm going to work my tail off to get there." Did you ever notice that you don't get there? You don't get there because you are not *here*. And you can't be there happily if you are not here happily, because you are only going to complain when you are over there. Guess who goes with you? The only person who was in all the circumstances. It's like when men talk about their last four wives as if they were the problem. What's the constant in all those relationships?

Living the quality of order means being fully alive and present to the current moment. We don't want to be caught up in the past or live in the future. However, reflecting on the past can give us a true experience of the order of our lives.

I often work with a process called the Intensive Journal, by Ira Progoff, who was one of my teachers and mentors and a student of

Carl Jung. He created a fabulous technique for journaling. It's not just normal journaling, where you write down what's going on every day. It requires a whole series of different tabs in a notebook and every tab represents different ways of looking through your life. You write in one tab and then you flip through to another; and in the flipping, your life starts integrating.

In one of the Intensive Journal processes, you do something called creating your Stepping Stones. No matter your age, you choose twelve events as the stepping stones of your life. What were the twelve most important events that made you who you are today? Could you write those down? Interestingly, if you do this a year later, or six months later, those twelve things often change. It's fascinating. I've done Stepping Stones almost every year of my life, and depending on where I am in my life, the stepping stones change. I've been in workshops where people who have three children don't include them. Their births were amazing experiences, maybe even traumatic. Some people even left out a marriage, because it was no longer the prime focus at the moment they were writing. Whenever I'd do it, I'd know when I was supposed to be moving, because when I'd write my stepping stones, they were the places I had lived.

If you read my resume, you'll notice that I have a varied, eclectic, unusual, and extensive background. I was a math major, and then I studied adult learning. Left brain, right brain—neither knew which one was calling at which time. I was in a convent, I was a computer

programmer, and I was an actress for a while. I did seminars. I did all
kinds of stuff. It was always challenging to write my resume. I'd go to
a headhunter and he would look at my resume and say, "Who are
you? No one person could have done this." One of the things that the
Intensive Journal did for me was give everything in my life a place.
The journal even has a place to look at your longings, your dreams,
your motives, and the causes you work for; all of that has a place. My
life all fit in this book and it made sense. It actually cross-referenced
each other. I began to see patterns. I began to see things. Recently, I
was in a class creating a Web site, and most people in the class with
me have no idea of what to do. I was a programmer once. Did I know
twenty-five years ago that I would need that skill today? Yes I did, I
guess. The soul within me knew every step of the way. There are no
accidents. You had a job somewhere along the line and wondered
what it was about. Very often, when you reflect on your life and look
at the whole, you can see the connections.

The Intensive Journal workshop meant a great deal to me. It
showed me that my life did have a perfect order; everything I had ever
done had a place. It had a place in the notebook and it had a place in
my life. It gave me a sense of the order of things and helped me realize
that the things that have happened *had* happened. Has this ever happened to you? Have you ever taken a job and then discovered that the
skills that you had developed long ago are now coming in handy?
Things you did that you didn't think you'd need and wondered why

you did that? Our lives aren't random. There is an order. When we stop and look at the current moment, we begin to reflect on the order of our lives.

We all tend to have a past that keeps us hanging on to yesterday. What is your story? "I never got an education; my parents didn't love me; I came from a dysfunctional family; I am the child of an alcoholic." Let go. Stop talking about it. Even if the past was the best days you ever had, give thanks for them and keep looking ahead.

Are you lost in the future, looking at what you do not yet have? Why not allow yourself to fully enjoy what you do have, rather than lament what has not yet come to be? Expectations are often the nemesis of appreciation. We get into the childish "I want" syndrome rather than allow ourselves to be "in gratitude for what is."

I was once in the presence of an Indian guru who asked his disciples what they would choose if they were offered—ten million dollars or ten children. Of course, most people shouted out, "Ten million," to which he replied, "You would be better off having ten children, because then you wouldn't always be wanting more."

I have come to realize that the very search for pleasure is often a denial of the depth and beauty of the moment. Instead, when we experience life with childlike freshness, amazement, and emptiness in our eyes, then life itself will reveal its mystery and fulfill our deepest longings.

Do you set goals and then focus on them to the point of allowing yourself to believe that "I'll be happy when....? When I lose the weight I gained, when I am in a committed relationship with the man I love, when I am producing x amount of income, when I'm...." You fill in the blanks, whether it's material, spiritual, or personal. Can you really believe that life is perfect just as it is, with every circumstance, every person, and yourself exactly where and who we are right now?

Having goals can tend to narrow our vision. What we need instead of goals is a true sense of direction, and instead of attachment, commitment. It's a subtle difference, but a major one. Then and only then will we balance having a vision and living in the now. Almost everyone I speak to has some goal or issue he is working on. I'd like to present an alternative view: allowing life to happen rather than making it happen. It's a delicate balance to truly love yourself exactly as you are at this moment, to love the one you're with.

A minister friend of mine told me a story about the man in her church who wanted to quit his job. She had told the class she was teaching to look in the mirror each day and say, "I love you just the way you are." He committed to it and did it for six months. Within that time, his company began to expand his responsibilities. Where before he worked alone, he now has twenty-five people directly reporting to him. His salary has multiplied considerably. His six months expanded into two years of this practice. He's a changed person.

Love the one you're with—yourself—now, and not when. Consciousness is all about being in the moment. It comes down to truly being present to whatever it is you are about at the moment. When you are truly focused, you begin to love whatever it is that you are doing. And you begin to hear the inner voice that more clearly guides you to do the perfect thing in the moment.

You can practice consciousness while cleaning the bathroom. A man I know found his mind kept wandering when he wanted to do a quick and dirty job. But when he focused on cleaning each tile and began to concentrate on that tile alone, he began to make a game of it and thoroughly enjoyed what would have been a distasteful task. I do this when I'm washing pots. I do about half of a really dirty pot and I want to stop and come back to it later. Focusing in the moment, doing one task at a time, allows me to finish far more and work half as hard in getting more done. As we learn to become more present in the moment, more conscious, events will begin to trigger just the reaction we need. The secret of dealing with any situation we want to change is to be in it but not buy into it, and not make it wrong or try to suppress it.

When we misidentify with the experience, our reactions dissolve. Resistance to reality disappears. When we feed into an emotion we intensify it, and when we tell ourselves we shouldn't feel that way, we suppress it. We do these things when we see our experiences as a threat, rather than accept all that comes as perfect for me right now.

We are truly free when we don't try to justify or find blame. The only way to become free from fears, compulsions, and addictions is to observe them, and love ourselves as we are in the moment and take full responsibility for them. Releasing the emotional need frees us to be in the present moment fully.

True trust is a willingness to accept whatever happens to us. The secret of life is developing a capacity to engage in it fully, moment by moment as it presents itself. No fight, no resistance. Even if you are currently facing a challenge, just accept the reality of it. Pain accepted always dissipates. When your car breaks down, think about how you will feel about it tomorrow. This, too, shall pass. No matter how real the moment feels or how deep the pain or joy, know what Scripture repeatedly says: "And it came to pass."

Whenever you find that you're not with the one you love, remember the song, and love where and who you are—the one you are with. Let go of the past. Release the future. Now is the only moment you have. Live it fully!

I received the following prayer from a colleague of mine, Dr. Tom Johnson. It's entitled "All Is in Divine Order," and it's the perfect way to close this chapter.

> The perfection and completeness of God always are. They are always in action and so God-action is forever establishing order and harmony. I am God's means to express Itself, and so order is always established through and by means of me. My each and

every thought is centered on the allness of God and Its divine order. All that I do creates and maintains order.

God lives by means of me in the eternal now, and that which is no longer required in my life I lovingly and joyfully release. The Self that I am creatively eliminates that which no longer plays a part in my unfoldment. The clutter of yesterday is gone and the order of today is established. All that needs to be done today by means of me is free to be done, because I am the clarity of knowing Who and What I really am today. Swiftly, easily, and correctly I move into action and order, divine order, is established. Fresh, new ideas are now free to come into my consciousness of order because I have released the old and made way for the requirements of today. All is in divine order.

Chapter 10
Peace

"Let it begin with me."

A woman was walking along the beach and found a bottle. She picked up the bottle and rubbed it until, naturally, a genie came out. The woman said to the genie, "Oh, good, do I get three wishes?"

The genie replied, "You know, that's an old myth. We genies have been hanging around for a long time and all we have left is one wish. You can only have one thing. What is it that you want?"

She didn't hesitate to respond, "I want peace in the Middle East. I'm tired of hearing stories of war. See this map? I want these countries to stop fighting with each other. I want all Arabs to love all Jews and all Americans and vice versa. I want this world to live in peace and harmony."

The genie looked at her and said, "Lady, be reasonable. These countries have been fighting for so many thousands of years. I'm out of shape. I've been in this bottle for centuries. I can't quite do that. I'm not that good. I don't think it can be done. Please make another wish and make it more reasonable."

The woman thought for a moment and said, "Well, I'm single and I've never been able to find the really right man. You know, one who is considerate and fun. One who likes to cook and do housecleaning. He's great in bed and he gets along well with my family. He doesn't watch sports all the time. He's faithful and he's handsome. That's what I'll wish for—a good man whom I can marry and make my partner."

And the genie replied, "Give me that map."

If you had only one wish, would it be for peace? What would peace look like? What would happen if we focused on that quality? What would a spiritual practice based in peace look like on a daily basis? But before we answer those questions, let's begin by defining peace.

The first definition that I resonate with is that peace is the *feeling* that accompanies knowing truth. (I am using the word *feeling* here as a deep belief, a deep knowing, a deep understanding that there is truth present.) When something is true you get that calmness in your stomach that says, "Ah, yes!" and that's when you know that you know something. It is the test that lets you know that you are following the right path, or what some might call God's will. How do you know when you know? It *feels* peaceful. When you are trying to make a decision, but you are not quite sure it is the right decision, you'll go down one path in your mind and it will get you all agitated. Then you go down another path in your mind until that feeling says, "Ah, yes!" and that's when you know.

What's it like when you *hear* truth? Do you feel peace when people are arguing? No. But, when you start hearing the truth, even if it is something you don't quite grasp yet, something in you just feels it; something in you knows. When you know something, that's pretty automatic, isn't it? It's not something you need to figure out. Peace is the natural state of our being, because the natural state of our being is to live in truth.

Peace is also an *experience*. It happens when everything is in perfect timing, just as it should be. This definition helps you see why you need to focus on this quality for a year. Accepting things as they are is peaceful. The minute we feel like we have to fix things we know that something is wrong. Is there anything in your life you are trying to fix or change? If so, you might be thinking, "This isn't right! It's got to be different." The minute we think it's got to be different, we lose our feeling of peace.

What if we become aware of that feeling and really begin to believe that there is a divine order to this universe? There is an infinite power in this universe and it knows exactly what needs to happen, exactly when it needs to happen. What if we become aware that nothing is apart from Go(o)d? If we really get that, then we stay in the experience of peace. The minute we feel as if something has to change, we lose peace. Peace doesn't mean that everything is going to go the way we like it. Peace doesn't mean that everything is necessarily "going well." Peace is the experience of *knowing* that there is a divine presence and a divine power and it is all good. And that *knowing* is underneath everything, even what may look like chaos on the outside. That's an important distinction.

Peace doesn't mean that when you say, "I choose peace," you suddenly get it. Why don't I experience peace at every single moment? There's a big difference between feelings and emotions. The war may rage. Things may happen. In fact, I've had a hard week. All the little stuff happened; every single thing that could have possibly caused me to lose my peace happened. Nothing major, thank goodness. Every phone call was somebody who was upset about something. And there were breakdowns—you know, those silly things that go wrong around the house. I had a choice, constantly, to go with how my emotions were carrying me at the moment or to go with the feeling of peace. I'm learning more and more that I can always make a choice for peace.

Peace may not be the immediate emotion. Our emotions happen automatically. We can't stop them. I don't know of anyone who wants to be emotionless. I remember once, many years ago, frantically saying to a therapist, "I think people who don't feel are better off."

She replied, "The depth of your pain is the depth of your joy. If you don't allow yourself to have these emotions, you can shut off all of life."

The beauty of life is that we can be in the middle of tears and still know peace. We have to get the understanding that peace is not the absence of emotion. Peace exists at the level of cause, not effect. That's real important to grasp, since it's at the heart of understanding this teaching and fully understanding the Law of Attraction. Everything is an inside job. If we wait for peace because of what is happening, we are allowing our lives to be dictated by what's outside of ourselves. Anything that happens in the universe can make us lose our peace. Well, that's not very powerful, is it? If we think that peace comes only when things are going well, then we are at the mercy of life, of all the things happening around us. If we remember that life happens as a result of what we choose, then we get to be at cause. Feelings can be like a radio station. If you do not like the station you are listening to, you can switch to another one, replacing a negative emotion with a positive one.

Sometimes, however, when you try to replace a negative emotion, the first one keeps coming back, which can be the cause of a struggle. You've probably had the experience of having an upsetting thought that you just couldn't let go. This is when it is important to recognize your innate capacity for being calm, for being compassionate, and living in peace.

The Vietnamese Buddhist monk Thich Nhat Hanh in *Creating True Peace* says

> This is your true nature, your Buddha nature, or the awakened nature inside you. When you bring to mind these qualities of great compassion and understanding, you acknowledge their presence within you and you immediately suffer less.... The Buddha nature is not an abstract notion. It is a reality you can touch and experience. Buddha nature exists in every cell of our body. The cells of our body aren't made up of only physical matter. Our bodies are matter; they are also a manifestation of consciousness.... Every cell of our body contains all the talents, wisdom, goodness, and happiness of the Buddha, and also all of our spiritual and blood ancestors. Of course, every cell also contains in it the seeds of hell, of violence, of jealousy, of anger, of other negative emotions. But we can practice so that hell does not overpower the energies of mindfulness, understanding and loving-kindness in us. When you are suffering, you forget your Buddha nature, your goodness, and believe that within you is only suffering, only fear, turmoil and hatred. Please, please, please remember to trust your Buddha nature.[1]

I would like to also share a passage from the private works of Joel Goldsmith. (These were taken from notes from a lecture that my friend Judy's aunt attended many years ago.) The following passage is the Christian version of Thich Nhat Hahn's Buddha nature:

> When you are going through a period of unhappiness, or illness, or lack of peace, or lack of prosperity or frustration, remember that this has nothing to do with your outer world. It's imperative that you grasp that. You'll be tempted to believe that your external world is causing the difficulty, that it is distracting you or causing you pain, but this is not so at all. If you can discern that this represents a battle going on within you, you will quickly achieve victory just through the ability to discern that no person or condition or situation is doing anything to you. This is the battle within you. Your higher self, whom you have embraced, the Christ, is seeking ascendancy over the mortal sense into which you were born. This is the Son of God in you struggling to come into manifestation and expression.[2]

When things are going wrong, when you are feeling a lack of peace, happiness, or prosperity, or feeling frustration or illness, instead of looking at the object out there as causing the pain, you need to know that the Buddha nature, or Christ being within you, that higher self within you, is longing to take over and to undo everything that is not like itself. The stuff showing up in your life gives you an opportunity to choose to live from that higher place. It has nothing to do with the stuff outside; it is all about a beautiful victory that you are being asked to participate in, what Goldsmith calls—"the Christ ascending in you." When you turn on the light, you begin to recognize that there is no darkness. The struggle is never against people or conditions or things. The struggle is within you, until your real self, your spiritual self, remembers its own truth. Then you might even find that this outer world is already heaven. When you are tempted to fight any false sense of disease, condition, lack, or limitation in any form, relax at once and realize that this is not true. Don't condemn yourself. Don't say, "Why is this happening to me?"

A lot of my coaching clients come to me wondering why they aren't "further along." That's what we do to ourselves. We say, "Why am I still "here" at this age?" As if "there" is a better place to be than "here." As if "there" is some place we are *supposed* to get to. We have made up some false beliefs that say, "By this age I ought to have this, and if I don't, something's wrong." Or, "I ought to be doing *this*, whatever *this* is." For all of us, "this" is better health, more money, better relationships, or something similar. We're putting it out to the universe and saying, "I'm not there!" Is anybody really there? Where is there? This is it? This *is it* … exactly where we are.

Goldsmith continues, "Every knee is going to bend; so let the battle rage and let the Christ come into ascendancy. You and I can do nothing about that. We can't make it so, and we can't hurry it."[3]

Do you want to hurry it? I do. I just want to get there. I want to be in my higher self at all times, in all places. Wouldn't that be nice?

That's where my fight is. It's not okay to be where I am, constantly, so I must let it be. All we can do is surrender and be as forgiving of ourselves as we are of our neighbor. The master teacher said, "Do not suppose that I have come to bring peace to the earth. I did not come to bring peace, but a sword" (Matt. 10:34). The Christ doesn't come to lift you up to a cloud nine existence. It comes to tear you away from that self which must die, one way or another. Even the good self has to die.

Goldsmith continues:

> When you are going through difficulties, it is so important to remember that it is the Christ that is doing it, not the devil, or Satan, or your ego, or your illness, or your domestic situation. None of that is true. It is the Christ. It is doing this in order to take you out of your fleshly peace, your temporal peace. Do not be afraid. It is I.[4]

What powerful words to let us know what is going on. The raging within us is the longing of our higher nature, the Christ self, the Buddha nature, that which is the true part of us, longing to come into total being. This is what drives our life. When we're fighting it, we're really saying, "I want to fix it; I want to find out," rather than, "I surrender to that which is in me already as peace. I surrender to that which is already the good."

Thich Nhat Hahn also said, "When I have a toothache, I discover that not having a toothache is a wonderful thing."[5] That is peace. As I mentioned earlier, I am writing one hundred things a day that I am grateful for. Today is day forty, so I've written four thousand things for which I am grateful. Some days I come up with being grateful for what is *not* happening. I'm grateful that "this" didn't happen this week. Think about that. When I don't have a toothache, I'm grateful. We can be grateful for so many things. It depends on what we put our focus on.

A common definition of peace says that it is a state of calm and quiet. It also says that it's the absence of war or strife. That's how we tend to look at peace at times. A mother tends to think of peace when all the children are in bed. A factory worker thinks of peace when the machinery stops and it gets quiet. We think that when something ends we have peace.

A wise old gentleman retired and purchased a modern home near a junior high school. He spent the first two weeks of his retirement in peace and contentment. Then a new school year began. The next afternoon, three young boys full of youthful, after-school enthusiasm came down his street beating merrily on every trash can they encountered. The crashing percussion continued day after day until the wise old man finally decided it was time to take action. The next afternoon he walked out to meet the young percussionists as they banged their way down the street. Stopping them he said, "You kids are a lot of fun. I like to see you express your exuberance like that. In fact, I used to do the same thing when I was your age. Will you do me a favor? I'll give you each a dollar if you'll promise to come around every day and do your thing."

The kids were elated and continued to do a bang-up job on the trash cans. After a few days the old-timer greeted the kids again, but this time he had a sad smile on his face. "The recession is really putting a big dent on my income," he said, "so from now on I'll only be able to pay you fifty cents to beat on the cans."

The noisemakers were obviously displeased, but they did accept his offer and continued their afternoon raucous. A few days later, the wily retiree approached them once again as they drummed their way down the street. "Look," he said, "I haven't received my Social Security check yet, so I'm not going to be able to give you more than twenty-five cents. Will that be okay?"

"A lousy quarter!" the drumbeaters exclaimed. "If you think we're going to waste our time beating those cans around for a quarter, you're nuts! No way, mister, we quit!"

And the old man enjoyed peace.

Peace is not the absence of noise necessarily. In the Bible, peace is far more of a positive quality than just the absence of something. When you translate the Hebrew word *shalom*, which we often call "peace," it means well-being, wholeness, and prosperity. When you say *Shalom* to someone, you're not simply saying peace, but you're saying all of the divine qualities. If you choose to focus on any of these qualities, you get them all. Whole being can't be separated. The whole point of the exercise of choosing qualities is that our minds can't focus on all of them all at once, so we choose one. In choosing peace, we have total well-being; we have total wholeness; we have prosperity as well.

How do we practice peace? I call it nonviolent living, and we can practice it in so many areas—individually, in our relationships, and in our world. What about nonviolent living with ourselves? How many people are "living driven"? We've got to get this done, we've got to do that thing, and the world is going to end if this doesn't happen. Can you see how that's violence? We are doing violence to ourselves. We were never meant to live at the pace that our modern society is calling us to live. Think about that. We have all these modern conveniences that are making it twice as hard for us to live at times. We have to acquire them and we have to maintain them. We have to do all these extra things.

Our forefathers gave us a challenge by talking about the pursuit of happiness, because that's what we do—pursue it continually—instead of accepting that it already is. I constantly say to people and to myself, "If amassing all these things and getting all these things done were really important and you were to die today, what would you take with you? What's really important? What do you really want? Where is your energy going?"

Consider all the overindulgence in our society. We're doing violence to ourselves when we overindulge. What about putting ourselves down? Most of us do violence to ourselves in the way we talk about ourselves, in the way we deal with ourselves, instead of seeing ourselves as made in the image of God. How would you treat someone if you knew that right through your front door was coming God itself right now? What would you do? How would you treat God? How would you experience God? That's the truth about who you and I are. We are individual expressions of God. Why aren't we treating ourselves as such? Look at the way we put ourselves down.

The practice of peace is looking in the mirror every day and saying, "I love you exactly as you are." If you haven't done it for a while, do it for a week. Look in the mirror and say, "I love you just the way you are." Let it be God's voice—that Christ nature that's trying to break through. Let the Buddha nature within you, your higher self, tell you what it thinks of you. Stand there and look in the mirror so you can hear it coming back.

Remember the song I mentioned in chapter 5, "How Could Anyone?" It makes most people I know cry when they hear it: "I love you. You are beautiful. I accept you as you are and as you are not." Say those words as you look in the mirror. "How could anyone ever tell you?" and that means *you*. Ending violence needs to begin with yourself. You need to find peace within yourself.

There's a peace inside of us that's unchanging, that's transcendent. I love the passage where Jesus said to his disciples, "Peace I leave with you; my peace I give you. I do not give to you as the world gives. Do not let your hearts be troubled and do not be afraid" (John 14:27). That was a promise. Perhaps you have not read the Bible in a long time. I recommend pulling it out and seeing the promises. "My peace I give to you" is yours already. Are you willing to accept it? Are you willing to take it, or are you bent on living the way you want to live, putting yourself down? "I have given you a gift. Do you want to use it or not?" That's what I hear happening here. So many people are, in effect, saying that they would rather live in pain and suffering, and would rather focus on the things that aren't working in life. Sometimes I think I do that. I wonder why I would rather focus on what's not working rather than on the gift that I've been given. Focusing on the divine qualities is an opportunity to focus on that gift that has already been given to us.

One of the things I do to practice peace when I'm not feeling it is to simply picture light going through my body. This is something you can do when there is pain in your body. Just allow the light to go through your body—especially to where there is pain—and watch what happens. That's the nature of light. God is light; you begin to feel that light, and you feel that peace. When we get who we really are, we begin to experience peace. The realization of our oneness with the omnipresence brings peace. All you have to do is remember the presence at the moment. And you know where the presence is? It's as close as your breath.

All the Buddhist teachings that I've read talk about two basic practices: breathing and smiling. Sometimes we look for something more profound, and the student in me wants to find the fifteen ways of.... But it's really simple. Allow yourself to breathe in peace. The Hebrew word, *Ruah*, the breath, is another word for spirit. When we remember that all there is in the universe is spirit, we can breathe that in. Then the minute we lose our peace over anything, all we need to do is stop and breathe. You cannot help but feel peace when you let that breath come in real deeply. Or smile, because you can't feel miserable when you are smiling. Can you think of your pain while you are smiling?

Try this experiment. Stand up, raise your hands high in the air, look up, and shout, "I'm depressed." You cannot physiologically feel depression when you are in a state, or position in your body, that says "victory." If I asked you right now to look depressed, you would know how to do it—your body slumps, your head goes down. All we need to do sometimes is change our physiology. Change the way you are sitting, or change the way you are standing. If you are lying in bed and feeling miserable, get up! This sounds ridiculous, but all the studies I've read about bringing peace in the world are about each person beginning to feel it. Begin changing your state. If it's a state of non-peace, find ways of changing that state. You cannot stay in depression when your lips are curled upward. It's impossible. The brain is wired to the body and the body tells it how to feel.

If you must be depressed, choose a good fifteen minutes to feel it, and feel it well. Write a letter to yourself and to your depression. Tell it you love it and want to hold on to it for at least fifteen minutes, and you are going to let yourself wallow in it as much as you know how. Otherwise, you will fight it constantly. So embrace it. This, too, is Go(o)d. And then change your state. It's not a matter of never having those emotions. Emotions show up. We don't want to fight them. That's what makes us human. We want to embrace them, accept them, allow them, and hold them—but not hold onto them. We have so many old beliefs that are keeping us back: beliefs about what we should be doing; beliefs about what is the right and perfect thing; beliefs that say, "This is the only way," or, "I'm not good enough." You can overcome those old beliefs by some simple practice.

"Peace is my gift to you." That's what the Christ said. When a famous poet was dying, his aunt Louise asked, "Have you made your peace with God?" He looked her right in the eye and said, "I didn't know we had ever quarreled." Wonderful!

The Dalai Lama wrote the foreword to Thich Nhat Hanh's book, *Peace Is Every Step*. In it he wrote, "Although attempting to bring about world peace through the internal transformation of individuals may seem difficult, it is the only way. Peace must first be developed within. I believe that love, compassion and altruism are the fundamental basis for peace. Once these qualities are developed within an individual, he or she is then able to create an atmosphere of peace and harmony. This atmosphere can be expanded and extended from the individual to his family, from the family to the community and eventually to the whole world."[6]

There's an old Chinese proverb: "When there's light in the soul, there is beauty in the person. When there's beauty in the person, there is harmony within the home. When there's harmony within the home, there's order in the nation. When there's order in the nation, there is peace in the world." Let there be peace on earth. Let it begin with me.

Another way to practice nonviolence toward others is seeing each person as if he or she were new every day. Two friends were walking through the desert. At a specific point on the journey, they had an argument, and one friend slapped the other one in the face. The one who got slapped was hurt, but without anything to say, he wrote in the sand, "Today, my best friend slapped me in the face."

They kept on walking until they found an oasis, where they decided to take a bath. The one who got slapped started drowning, and the other friend saved him. When he recovered from his fright, he wrote on a stone, "Today my best friend saved my life."

The friend who slapped and then saved his best friend asked him, "Why, after I hurt you, did you write in the sand, and now you write on a stone?"

The other friend, smiling, replied, "When a friend hurts us, we should write it down in the sand, where the winds of forgiveness are in charge of erasing it away. When something great happens, we should engrave it in the stone of the memory of the heart, where no wind can erase it."

We do violence by remembering hurts from the past. It is challenging for us to look at each other and not remember something that happened yesterday or a month ago. We hold onto those things and see each other as if we were that person still, and we don't give ourselves the opportunity to grow. George Bernard Shaw put it wonderfully when he said, "The only man who behaves sensibly is my tailor; he takes my measures anew each time he sees me, while all the rest go on with their old measurements and expect them to fit me."

What if we really began to listen to one another? Here's a practice I decided to adopt, and I invite you to join me: deep listening. When another person begins to speak, rather than react or say anything, just listen. Let the speaker finish; let him say what he is saying. Deep listening is a way of showing that we truly believe the other person is new at every moment.

We have all kinds of ways to bring peace in the world. We can join marches and demonstrations. We can get involved in politics. All that is good if that is where you are led. But perhaps the best way is to do was written on a greeting card I received which quotes Thomas Merton as saying: "If you are yourself at peace, then there is at least some peace in the world. Then share your peace with everyone, and everyone will be at peace."

Chapter 11
Power

"All things are possible with God;

all things are possible for me."

Perhaps one of the least understood divine qualities that we humans share is that of power. In our society there is a lot of misunderstanding about what power is, and what it isn't; and who has it and who doesn't; as well as what it means to be powerful. In spiritual circles, we often hear people say, "I gave away my power." I've even said to people, "Who are you giving your power to?" But this isn't the power we speak of when we speak of power as a divine quality. If it's a divine quality, it is unchanging; it cannot be given away. It's not something that is here today and gone tomorrow; it always was and always is.

As children, we probably all heard that God is omnipresent, meaning present everywhere (even in us); and omniscient, meaning all-knowing; and omnipotent, meaning all-powerful. The image these words conjure up is one of a Santa Claus who is pointing a finger saying, "You better watch out!" This powerful being knew everything you were doing and was going to punish you.

That's not the power we are addressing here either. The definition I am using is: power is the possession of control, authority, or influence; the physical, mental, or spiritual ability to act or produce an effect. I hope that you will have a deeper understanding of the true meaning of this kind of power as you read this chapter.

Let's try for a moment to understand the power of the divine and then look at the implications it might have for our understanding of our own power. This is more a theological reflection on power, rather than on the kinds of power I used to teach about in my university sociology or management classes. The nature of divine power is consistently ambivalent. There are two values or two senses of the power of the divine coexisting. One is what we think of as "power over"—the power to control other people or things and direct them to do one's will. The other we refer to as "power with"—the power in working with others, or the cocreative process.

I'd like to spend more time here on power over, because at first it might sound negative. Most people have had some negative experience with feeling controlled and manipulated. By virtue of the fact that we are born small beings, someone bigger than we are is always controlling what we do.

David Hawkins, medical doctor and author of the book *Power vs. Force*, defines *force* as when we attempt to get someone else to do what we want, or attempt to make the universe work in a certain way by our efforts or prayers.[1] (Have you noticed that when we pray, we often tell God what we want done, that we are directing?) Hawkins says that we are using force rather than true power. True power takes into account responsibility; we get that we are not victims, and that no one or nothing can control us. We come into our power when we start to recognize that. If we are still living as if other people hold the strings, or even as if a god out there holds the strings, then we don't understand the power that is ours.

In chapter 6, we talked about responsibility as the ultimate in knowing that we are free. When we understand that, we also get to experience the true power—the power of God over the world, and our power to direct our world and the conditions of our lives. The first definition of power then, "power over," is the ability to direct the world around us. That sometimes does mean controlling the forces of nature, other people, or, in a real sense, ourselves: our emotions, our thinking, and therefore our experiences. We direct by the power of our intention.

A friend of mine, Betty, told me a story that illustrates power that we seldom realize we have. Her mother had just made her transition in Michigan, where it was winter and about seven degrees below zero. Betty asked for a sign to know her mom was okay. She forgot to tell her mom that before her mom died, and she had no idea what to expect but knew that she would see something. On the day of her mother's death, she found a ladybug sitting on a light fixture. Betty's mother visited each of her daughters later that week and they all saw four or five ladybugs in the house—in the middle of winter in Michigan!

Power over when viewed as a divine quality is a good thing. There is no greater power than aligning with my divine intention and my divine self. Intention is an inside job. We've heard it said, "God can only work for us by working through us." There is nothing God can do without working through us. To know that "I Am cause to my creation," is the ultimate power.

People often speak of miracles by saying that they experience the power of God as if it were beyond anything we can readily imagine or experience. But the truth is, as we develop the receptivity to owning God's power as our own and start to realize that it is within each one of us, we begin to develop what has been called the mental equivalent of that which we want to create. We get the knowing that it is already ours.

I can remember the first time that I did a spiritual mind treatment, or affirmative prayer. I remember feeling, "Wow! What I am speaking is really going to happen. In fact, it is happening as I speak." If you have done this, do you remember the first time that happened to you? We get that there is a power that we can use. We get to the knowing and owning that it is already ours. That's when we come to see the miraculous as the ordinary in our experience. Do you really know how powerful you are? Do you know that the same power that is "out there" is in each one of us?

A woman whom I had not met before once came to see me. She had been to our church only once, so she didn't really know any of the things I teach. She started telling me about a serious problem she was having with cancer. As she was speaking, I got real clear that her problem had nothing to do with cancer. She began to share more and more, and began to tell me about the fact that she had been and was still in a very abusive relationship. She began to say, "I think that's the issue. I'm terrified of stepping out on my own. Where would I ever get insurance? Who would take care of me?" (Not that he was taking care of her!)

I just listened and didn't say a word to this woman. She sat there and looked at me and said, "I think I brought this into my life." I would never have said to her, "You brought cancer into your life." I don't believe in that. You don't want to look at people and say, "You have a cold—you must be doing 'xyz.'"

"But," she said to me, "I'm beginning to realize that my allowing these experiences is actually causing and creating my experiences."

She was sitting in a chair and she suddenly jumped up out of the chair and said, "I'm powerful, aren't I?"

I said, "Yes, you are."

Then she said, "If I can do that, I can change my life." She looked at me and started to cry, saying, "I've been through years and years of therapy and I've never felt free. I'm free."

I didn't do a thing. She heard herself, and in my presence, while I held a conscious space, she began to see her own power.

For all of us who are creating muck in our lives, see how powerful we are? Look what we can do. When you can understand this, then you can transform the situation. We've got to be really careful that we don't think that there is a God out there who has a will and desire for our lives that is separate from what we want. We've all heard in the past, "It must be God's will." Have you noticed that usually refers to anything we'd label as "bad"? Nobody ever says it must be God's will when everything is wonderful. I've come to understand that we have to always look for what will make us feel good. Nothing is more important.

In the moment, when you speak a word, "will that make you feel good?" When you go to do something, "will that make you feel good?" When we do this, but if we believe that there is a will of God somewhere out there and we've got to find it, no wonder we don't feel our power. We think we have to get aligned with something outside ourselves. "There must be some secret that I don't know," we say, "and maybe if I sit here long enough and work to figure it out, I'll get in touch with what God wants." We're too afraid of knowing our own power. When we speak our word and know very clearly what it is that we want, we can create it. Most of us are too afraid of that, and yet that's the truth. So many of us, myself included at times, still think there is some will out there that maybe I'm pleasing. I'll give you an extreme example of this told to me by a colleague from the West Coast.

A man once starved to death in his pickup in the mountains. He had become stuck in a snowdrift in a mountain pass and sat in that truck for nine weeks waiting for someone to rescue him as he prayed, "If it is the Lord's will." Throughout that time he kept a diary and wrote letters to loved ones. It is clear from those diaries that this man believed God caused him to get stuck in that snow and that he would get out only if it was God's will. For more than two months, he sat there wondering whether or not it was God's will for him to live. Finally, he died of starvation.

When someone finally found him, he was only a one hundred-yard walk away from a clear road he could have used to find help. One hundred yards of snow and a wrong idea about God stood between this man and life. Starvation didn't kill that man. His theology did.

God's will for us is our good, and only more good. Not "for your own good"—like you'll get locked in the closet and be fed spinach. That's not what I mean. We were given the power to create good. We get to the root of really understanding power over when we start to reflect on the power of our own word.

The first and foundational manifestation of God's "power over" is creation, particularly as formulated in the doctrine of "*creatio ex nihilo*," created out of nothing. God speaks, and all that is comes into being. Go back and read the book of Genesis. It tells you about this power. God's power here is absolute. Creation, for God, is effortless. There are no challenges, threats, or obstacles to God's power. The word of God is law everywhere. There is one power, and as we come to realize that God makes human creatures in the image and likeness of itself, then we share this power over.

In the book of Genesis we read, "Then God said, 'Let us make man in our image, in our likeness, and let them rule over the fish of the sea and the birds of the air, over the livestock, over all the earth, and over all the creatures that move along the ground'" (Gen. 1:26). In creating humans, God empowered us by giving us life and by sharing dominion with us. This is the power we have to transform our own lives.

I've noticed that power feels like work. I'm not sure when I first put those two thoughts together: "If I'm going to be powerful, it means I'm going to have to be out there working." I'm learning a lot lately about relaxing and allowing—and I'm coming to see that transformation is not about working on myself. If you are "working on yourself," stop it. It's not about working with the emphasis on *work*. It is not about doing things the right way. (Are you still trying to figure out what way is the *right* way?) Someone in one of my seminars the other day kept asking, "Am I getting this right?" My students keep asking me, "Am I praying right?" As if you can pray wrong!

I recently heard about a Jewish woman who was attending both temple and a New Thought church. Her reasoning? She wanted to make sure she got it right. What if *they* were right?

I've been listening to a song each morning, by the talented singer/songwriter, Lisa Umberger, and a line in it says, "And we do not have to work for it, and we do not have to pray for it, and we do not have to struggle, for we are joy and we sing because we're joy." Isn't that wonderful? I love that song. We need that as a mantra to understand that this power isn't about force. It's not about making things work. It's not about figuring things out. It's allowing them to be.

My chief excuse for not getting this message out there in the past has been that I don't have the energy to do all the work it takes to do this. In writing this book on the twelve divine qualities, I'm finding that as I allow God to do this work as me, I have more energy than I have had in years. It's been amazing. The key here is to allow what is already within me to come forth. That's power; the other way of making everything in life work is force. I know how to make things work.

I made a business work. I made my students work. Force seems to work for a time, but it is exhausting. Power, on the other hand, is about allowing.

As we come to realize that this power over is our inheritance, we see that we exercise power over the way God showed us in Genesis—by the word. The key to transforming any experience in life is through the spoken word, as well as our internal words. Watch your words. My parents used to say to me when I was young, "Never say anything you wouldn't want printed in the newspaper." What is it that you would like to have printed in the newspaper? Say only those words. Start listening to yourself and noticing what you say. Your words reflect your belief in both power over and power with. Our every word is actually a prayer. What we speak into the universe, we eventually see manifested in our lives. This is an experience of true "power over." Recognizing that we can speak words that are uplifting and healing for others is part of power with.

A few years ago, I was teaching a group of preteens, and the only way I could keep their interest was to show them some kinesiology. For example, it's guaranteed that if I ask you to stand and hold your arm out and think negative thoughts about yourself, your arm would go totally weak. And when I ask you to think empowering thoughts about yourself, your body gets strong, without resistance. There was one boy in the group whom everyone hated. He came up to the front of the room and I asked the group to think positive thoughts about him. This startled them; they all giggled or laughed and said, "No way," But they finally did, so we tried an experiment. I got them to stand in a line and reach out and hold each other's hands, and I asked the whole group to think positive thoughts about little Joey. When I touched the last person at the end of the line, everybody was strong. When the group began to think negative thoughts about Joey, however, everybody went weak. And then I took just one person up and said, "You think negative thoughts about someone else for a moment," and the kid's arm went weak. I didn't have to say another word.

It's not just what we think about ourselves; it's what we think and speak about everyone else that is an indication of our power or our weakness.

A ministerial colleague, Rev. Judith Churchman, tells the story of years ago in *Creative Thought Magazine*, when she first found the Science of Mind teaching and philosophy. She had a small child named Derik, who had a lot of illness. He was a hyperactive two-year-old with allergies who had endured numerous hospitalizations. She was hypervigilant and constantly worried about his health.

As her study progressed in Science of Mind classes, she saw how well-meaning parents, through their constant worrying, often help create poor health in their children; the very thing they are trying to avoid. She said that idea hit her like a ton of bricks. "We worried about Derik's health all the time," she wrote. "That's all we were thinking about." She and her husband decided to quit doing and saying things that added to Derik's self-image as a sickly child. For example, he would say things like, "Mommy, can I drink milk today or will it make me sick?" They decided to treat him like a healthy child and do their best to stop worrying about him.

Judith told him every night when she tucked him in what a strong, healthy boy he was. When he did get sick, she assured him he was a fast healer and could send the "disease" away. He believed her unquestioningly, as young children do. Within one year of consciously speaking differently, Derik was a different child. In fact, he did not see a doctor for two years until he had to have a checkup to start kindergarten. Derik is now a six foot three inch healthy, handsome young man of thirty. What power and influence we have on one another!

In the first chapter of John's Gospel we read, "In the beginning was the Word, and the Word was with God, and the Word was God.... Without Him was not any thing made that was made" (vv.1–2). What does that mean? How are you God? With every single word. My name, LaMotta, means "the word."

Do I speak the words that reflect the divine pattern? What are my words empowering? Am I empowering sickness and disease? Am I empowering lack and limitation by talking about it and claiming it? Whatever I say, I am claiming it is so.

I used to give scholarships to my classes all the time because I didn't think some people could afford to come to class. I thought I was doing it out of the generosity of my heart, and I was; but I had a sense that "this person won't be able to afford this." Do you want someone thinking that about you? That's not the consciousness you want your minister holding for you. So, I stopped giving scholarships!

Think about what we do to one another. "Oh, this person can't do that, so I better help him." How do we view one another? Never say anything about yourself or anyone else that you don't want to see realized in life.

Imagine that a Dictaphone was strapped on your shoulders the first thing tomorrow morning and you carried it with you all day until the last thing tomorrow night. It recorded every word you said, and then was repeated to you. You might be a little embarrassed. More than that, those words are creating your life. Never forget that the circumstances of your life tomorrow are molded by your mental conduct of today.

Using this power is about speaking the word for your desires. Talk about what you want, not about what you don't want. That's an easy phrase to say, but a challenge sometimes to live. We more often talk about what isn't. That's the whole point of this book on the divine qualities. Let's not focus on the goals we can't have or don't think are possible. Sometimes deep down we set goals, knowing that we set them before and they just haven't worked. "Well, I'm going to try one more time," we say. "This time I'm going to make it." And the reason we don't make it is because we are focused on what we don't have. Every time you focus on a goal, even one that looks good, you are focused on something that isn't in your life. So you are creating more of what isn't.

We want to focus more on the quality we want to experience; the more we focus on the quality, the more change we'll see. As you start focusing on power, watch yourself manifest power. Watch everything start happening as you say, rather than focusing on what's not there. Our words really have power for ourselves, and they have power for another.

A group of frogs was traveling through the woods, and two of them fell into a deep pit. All the other frogs gathered around the pit. When they saw how deep the pit was, they told the two frogs that they were as good as dead. The two frogs ignored the comments and tried to jump up out of the pit with all of their might. The other frogs kept telling them to stop, that they were as good as dead.

Finally, one of the frogs took heed to what the other frogs were saying and gave up. He fell down and died. The other frog continued to jump as hard as he could. Once again, the crowd of frogs yelled at him to stop the pain and just die. He jumped even harder and finally made it out. When he got out, the other frogs said, "Did you not hear us?" The frog explained to them that he was deaf. He thought they were encouraging him the entire time!

A little caveat: be careful who you let in on your dreams. We need to take seriously what other people think about us, not in a neurotic sense or acting out of what other people may think. What you think of me is still none of my business; but what you think of me helps create who I am. Remember the kinesiology example. I don't want people saying about me, "Oh, that poor thing; she can't do this." You don't want people to send negative energy about you. Share only with people who aren't going to scream "frog language" at you. Or if they do, be deaf to it. It's challenging to be deaf to words out there. Learn who you can share your dreams with, who you can talk to and tell your visions to. You want the power in their thinking to support the power in your own.

The frog story teaches two lessons. First, there is power of life and death in the tongue. If you control your tongue, you control your whole life. What are you speaking about? What are you allowing yourself to say about yourself or others? Whatever I say about another can either destroy that person or bring life. We have the power. It's not just given to kings and presidents. It's not the power that some people possess and others don't.

Second, there is a power for good in the universe, and you can use it. When we understand that we are totally responsible for our lives, *anything* is possible. When we really get that, we can speak our word and absolutely know that whatever we declare with conviction is so. That's why at our church we end our prayers with, "And so it is." That's not just a nice little phrase. We are not questioning whether a God out there might deem us worthy and grant us this request, but we see it as done, and we allow it to unfold in its perfect time. We are using this power all the time. We use it by our word, whether it is positive or negative. It goes forth with all the power behind it, every word we speak. So we should choose our words wisely.

Chapter 12
Unity

"There is only one of us."

What I am about to attempt to describe in this chapter is virtually an impossible task. We live in a dualistic world. Mystics tell us—and some people at times have had glimpses—of the experience of unity. But it is impossible to describe unity. Any discussion of unity is inherently flawed. We can't capture unity in words because words are dualistic; they have a beginning and an ending, and they are each limited to expressing one particular concept that is often interpreted differently by each person who hears them.

In mathematical terms, unity and infinity are one and the same, and you can't contain infinity in any word or symbol, although people have tried and then built whole systems of belief in the attempt.

As an aside, I decided to study mathematics when I went to college and graduate school, because I was intrigued with the concept of infinity as a child. (I was a unique child!) I thought that the study of mathematics would lead me to better understand infinity and, therefore, unity. Hopefully, you'll see through this chapter that leaving our minds open is one key way to come to unity.

You can't get to unity by understanding it. Unity can only be "known" through becoming it. And when you are unity, you don't need to describe anything. In fact, when you are it, you have no awareness of anything else to be described!

Despite these limitations, playing around with the concept of unity with our dualistic minds can be helpful and rewarding. As I said, it can help make the mind more flexible because it challenges many of our assumptions. Perhaps a good definition of enlightenment is to lose our inflexibility about things. That's good homework for this week; find the places you are inflexible. Just begin by noticing them and bit by bit challenge what you believe to be true. Begin to be open to trying on another way of thinking.

Unity is, in fact, the ultimate aim of our life and, at the same time, the essence of who we already are. So, despite the fact that it is hard to talk about, I will continue and attempt to keep this discussion practical.

First, I assume that if you are reading this message it is because you seek enlightenment. Enlightenment can be defined as liberation from dependence on any form. We're going to see later that the state of consciousness we have in duality is based on separation, but in unity is quite dependent.

Our sense of ourselves, our "I am," comes from identification with certain forms. We even define ourselves by the things we don't identify with as much as those that we do. We can say, "This is my body," for example, only by not identifying with all the other bodies around us. Our very identity is defined by exclusion.

We think we are both spiritual and physical beings. We talk about these as if they are mutually exclusive. The truth, however, is that there is no separation, and physical is not opposed to spiritual. All that exists is a creative expression of the prime or first cause of all creation. Science tells us that the essence of all created things is of one source.

I often teach that the substance from which things are created, the process through which they are created, and the form they express as—or that which is created—are all one and the same. Native Americans of the Lakota tribe say of all of life, "*Mitakuye Oyasin*"; we are all related. On the human level, that means that I am you and you are me. There is only one of us. The practical question then, is, why can't we all get along?

As humans, we live on a dualistic plane. That means we see, perceive, and experience everything in opposites. Things, people, and situations are always either/or: good or bad, right or wrong, life or death. When we live in the consciousness of unity, there are no opposites. There is no good or bad, no right or wrong, no life or death. There is only good, only right, only life.

The mystics of all religions teach that the good, or right, or life that exists on the unified plane of consciousness somehow combines both aspects of things that we experience in our usual dualistic way of life. But in the unified state of mind, the opposites no longer conflict with one another. To live in a unified state, in absolute reality, is bliss, unlimited freedom, fulfillment, and the unlimited realization of potentials that people call heaven or samadhi or nirvana, depending on your background.

Of course, this is not a place in time or space, but a state of consciousness. The unified state of consciousness is a question of understanding or as I often term it, "knowingness." Unity is our natural state. It is only when we forget that truth and begin to live as if on a dualistic plane that life seems to give us continuous problems. Think about this: conflicts only come about when you think that something can have an opposite. That's what creates all of our tensions, our disagreements, and our wars. This is, in fact, the human predicament.

No matter how oblivious or how unconscious we may be of it, there is a part of us—our real self or true self—which lives in a unified state of mind, which expresses, manifests, and is the unified principle. We know this must be so because for all of us, while we are experiencing conflicts, we are also experiencing a deep longing for a different way of experiencing. We yearn for the freedom, the bliss, and the mastery of life that feeling separate can never bring.

Here's where it gets tricky. The longing in us is misinterpreted by the personality part of us. It is misinterpreted partly because it is an unconscious yearning for what is usually termed as "happiness" or "fulfillment." It is only by coming to see that there are no opposites that the struggle, effort, fight, tension, conflict, anxiety, or fear disappears. The simplest way to experience unity in all of its forms is to *get* that there are no opposites. Let me demonstrate this with a familiar problem.

Think about the last time you had an argument with someone—say, an innocent quarrel with a partner or a friend. Weren't you convinced that you were "right"? Therefore, your partner or friend had to be "wrong." On the dualistic plane, remember, life can only be either/or. Have you ever noticed when you are in an argument that the outcome seems to matter more than the particular issue? Usually, if you stop and observe the emotions involved, they often have no relationship to the issue at stake. We are seldom upset at what is happening at the moment, but rather because it triggers a memory of an experience or emotion from the past.

We sometimes find ourselves arguing over things as if they were a life or death issue. Although you may think this is irrational on a conscious level, unconsciously being wrong truly means being dead, for being wrong means to be denied by the other. This is the important point. On the dualistic plane, our sense of identity is associated with the other person and not with our real self.

As long as we experience ourselves as only the outer self or physical self, we must depend on others. Hence, a slight quarrel becomes truly a matter of life or death, which explains the intensity of emotions and the intensity of proving we are right and the other person is wrong.

In any issue you happen to be involved in, as long as you feel that you must win, then something you believe is so! While what the other believes or thinks is not so, you are deeply involved in the world of duality, and therefore in constant strain and suffering, conflict and confusion. The more you fight in this way, the greater the confusion becomes.

We have come to believe that life is divided into two opposites, one being adhered to as the "right idea," the opposite aspect being declared as the "wrong idea." In reality, they both complement one another. Groucho Marx can teach us something about thinking only our way is right. On http://www.brainyquote.com he is quoted as saying, "Those are my principals; if you don't like them, well, I have others."

A teacher was explaining this concept to small children. She had two students who were always arguing. One day she took out a mask that had two faces, red on one side and green on the other. She had the students stand on either side of the mask and tell everyone what color he saw. Of course, one insisted that the face was green and the other red. She then had them switch sides. They were both right; they were simply seeing from the different points of view.

When something is seen from above, from the unified plane of truth and fulfillment, the two seeming opposites are not separate at all. They complement each other. There can only be "enemies" on a dualistic plane of consciousness. There is no known drug that can cure the premature formation of opinions.

Have you ever noticed that the more you attempt to prove someone wrong, the more friction exists, and the less you actually get what you thought you would obtain by proving yourself right in the first place? You see, what we deep down believe is that by proving ourselves right and the other person wrong, the other will finally accept and love us again and all will be well. Isn't that ironic? We all just want to be loved and accepted. We identify with our beliefs and ideas, and so when someone disagrees, it's as if he has denied our existence.

So how *do* you handle differences in opinions, beliefs, and ideas? Many of us think we are faced with the alternative of either having to give in, in order to appease the other and avoid damage for ourselves, or to continue fighting. But if we are still convinced of a right versus a wrong, and we give in, we'd lose our self-respect. If we think that the only two alternatives are fighting or submitting, we are bound to create tension, anxiety, and inner and outer conflicts.

When we take the high road to the unified plane, we discover that there is always truth at both ends. A couple of years ago I found

myself in constant disagreement with someone, and I hated the feeling. The way I finally decided to handle it was to begin to notice
when I was about to argue a point, and then to pause and really listen.
I then would say, usually just to myself, "That's interesting. I wonder
what experience that person must have had to believe what she is now
saying." And when I was able to really do that—which now is much
more of a habit—I could actually begin to see that there was another
side. That's how I was able to come to see that there is no right and
wrong, or good or bad, because it's all good.

When we seek this truth deep inside, we begin to approach our
real self and begin to experience unity. This simple act of seeking the
truth has several prerequisites, the most important of which is the
willingness to relinquish what we hold onto—whether a belief, a fear,
or a cherished way of being. When I say relinquish, I merely mean to
question it and to be willing to see that there is more beyond your
own outlook and convictions. I think that's what Jesus must have
meant when he said, "The truth will set you free" (John 8:32). Truth
is never either/or. To experience unity, we need to stop believing in
opposites. Imagine what your life would be like if you were never
opposed to anyone or anything.

Ask yourself, "What are the things I am opposed to? What in me
needs to think that my way is right? Is it my need for attention? Is my
identity so wrapped up in my opinions that I think if someone dis-

agrees that I am negated? Do I think I need to compromise to be loved?"

The only way you can truly enter into the unitive state of life, in which you can truly be the master, is to no longer need to triumph, to win, to be separate, to be special, to be right, to have it your way. We begin to experience true unity by finding and discovering the good in all situations, whatever they are, whether we deem them good or bad, right or wrong. This does not mean resignation, nor does it mean fearful giving in or weakness. It means going with the stream of life and coping with what is as yet beyond our immediate control, whether or not it is according to our liking.

It also means accepting where you are and what life is about for you at this moment. It means being in harmony with your own inner rhythm. This will open the channel, so that total self-realization will take place. When you begin to accept that in yourself, you move toward greater tolerance of others. Tolerance can be a good first step; it is the capacity for or practice of recognizing and respecting the opinions, practices, or behavior of others.

But why just tolerate? Why not celebrate? The paradox in all of this is that unity is experienced by the embracing and celebration of diversity. The tag line that describes my personal mission in life is: "*Celebrating Uniqueness and Recognizing Oneness.*" These are big concepts; the one and the many, duality and unity. Practically speaking, there is no such thing as opposites. There is no either/or, good or bad, right or wrong. It's all God.

So join me as I pray:

> I stand in the knowing that there is but one—one presence, one power, one God, one truth—and that each and every one of us is that. I now accept and know with the fullest knowing of my being that there can be no opposites. There can be no opponents. There can be no we or they, theirs or ours, yours or mine. There is only one of us. I see and know today in a fuller way the truth of unity. I see and respect the fullness of diversity. I now let go of any need to be right, of any insecurity that I may not be loved or accepted. I stand in the truth of who I am. I claim this truth as truth, and I see a world embracing this unitive consciousness. We are one. There is no duality; there is only unity. I claim it. I am it. I rejoice that this is so. And with a grateful heart, I allow this truth to be. And so it is.

Chapter 13
Wholeness

"The answers to every question

lie within the questioner."

This chapter's divine quality is wholeness, and I have two definitions for it. The first is "an unbroken completeness or totality," and the second is "a state of robust good health." I'll attempt to address both briefly by first saying that our spiritual wholeness *is* the source of our physical health. I like to think of spiritual wholeness as recognition of sufficiency or "enoughness."

Most of us spend a good deal of our lives trying to fix ourselves as if we were broken or damaged goods. Notice how many people talk about "working" on themselves—as in, "This is what I'm working on right now." People tell me this all the time. Deep down, I think a lot of us believe that we are flawed; that someday someone is going to find out that something is really wrong with us. We've kept it secret long enough. I thought that for a long time in my life. Fortunately, I no longer think that way, but a lot of my coaching clients come to me with this belief.

Maybe this thinking comes from hearing the word *no* so much when we were young. I once heard that the average person grew up hearing *no* a thousand times a day. Think about it. Almost everything you attempted to do as a little tyke, someone said, "No, don't go there, and don't do that." After a while you begin to think that something's wrong with you. "Everything I think I'm supposed to do, they tell me not to do." Just being born and growing up in a normal childhood is a confusing state.

Or maybe it comes from all the advertisements that tell us we will be okay when we use the right deodorant, or when we use the pill the ad is pushing. "Call your doctor and see if you can use...." Most of the time the ad doesn't even tell you what the pill is for, but the assumption is something is wrong with your life and you need it in order for your life to be okay. We are bombarded with that message constantly.

As I've previously stated, the goal-setting syndrome says, "Always strive for more, or at least better." This contributes to our belief that we must be flawed. Still, I admit that I believe in goal-setting; not because I think we need to get better than we are and work hard and strive to make it so, but because I believe that spirit/God/itself is continual self-expression. The more we self-express, the more we emulate God, which is who we are in the first place. Growth is about becoming more of who we already are. That's the whole point of living from these qualities. They are our inherent nature. This is who we are, and we need to grow into this if we don't yet believe it.

We are continually prodded to become *all* we are capable of being. There's always more. But we need to be careful that we allow ourselves to grow because we need to, not simply because we can. Here's a perfect example of the silliness of more, better syndrome:

The rich industrialist from the north was horrified to find the southern fisherman lying lazily beside his boat, smoking a pipe.

"Why aren't you out fishing?" said the industrialist.

"Because I have caught enough fish for the day," said the fisherman.

"Why don't you catch some more?"

"What would I do with them?"

"You could earn more money," was the industrialist's reply. "With that you could have a motor fixed to your boat and go into deeper waters and catch more fish. Then you would make enough to buy nylon nets. These would bring you more fish and more money. Soon you would have enough money to own two boats—maybe even a fleet of boats. Then you would be a rich man like me."

"What would I do then?" asked the fisherman.

"Then you could *really* enjoy life."

"What do you think I am doing right now?"[1]

There's a delicate balance between continually opening ourselves to be more and knowing that where we are already is perfect, whole, and complete. Wholeness, in this sense, means nothing is missing.

Let's talk about perfection for a moment. Society tells us that perfection is having everything the exact way *we* want it to be. Perfection, in this sense, means meeting our every expectation. The meal was perfect. The show was perfect. Simply put, they met our expectations. Now, that mentality will get you in trouble quickly. Very few things, if any, ever meet our expectations, and expectation is often the cause of our dissatisfaction with what already is.

In a spiritual sense, perfect, whole, complete means that life is a perfect manifestation of all of our thoughts and beliefs. Within every seed there is a perfect fruit. In his book, *Five Steps to Freedom*, Dr. John Waterhouse puts it wonderfully: "Ours is not to force the world into a submission of perfection, but rather to become ever more aware of the presence of Spirit in everything that we see, hear, taste, smell, feel, and know. Perfection is something of which to become aware, not something to achieve."[2]

We are, in fact, already a holy people. Holiness is a derivative of wholeness and holiness, and in its deepest essence, means dealing with reality, or dealing with what is so. Wholeness or holiness then becomes the state of being truly present wherever we are. When we do that, we begin to see that perfection is the norm. Anything we give our full attention to becomes perfect. Try it. The next time you are doing something you usually don't enjoy and wish you were elsewhere or doing something else, stop and fully focus on what you are doing and where you are. One of my students said she practiced this while washing dishes and it actually became pleasurable. Focus your full attention on whatever you are doing—perhaps paying bills or whatever chore you'd rather not be doing. You'll find that you come into stillness and peace and can actually begin to enjoy what you are doing. It's the continual wishing that something else were so right now that disturbs us and makes us feel less than whole. It's not what you are doing that's the problem; it's where your mind is going. "I wish I weren't doing this." When you cut that out, you come back to the perfection.

When we practice being totally present we begin to live in a constant state of gratitude. There's no better way to live. When we practice being totally present, we let go of distractions from the present moment. Distractions from the present moment are a way of being ungrateful for what is. The opposite of gratitude is criticism, and whenever we fail to focus on what we are doing, we are in effect criticizing it by wanting to do something else. When we are criticizing anything, we can't also feel gratitude. Almost all our unhappiness and suffering comes from thinking that we don't have something or someone that we think we should have right now. In other words, expectations. We should be in another place, doing another thing. It's what we think we should be doing, or what we think we should be having that's causing all our suffering. *All of it.*

This, of course, applies to our physical bodies as well. Often when we speak of wholeness we think in terms of being vibrantly healthy, and that is the second definition. But we need to be careful of a trap here as well. This is something I learned from a yoga master years ago. We used to do yoga postures in which we stayed in the posture for five minutes at a time. Trust me, after that long, the body starts to respond—usually with deep pain. But one day the master said, "Change the label of pain to sensation."

What would happen if we decided that any pain we experience—emotional, spiritual, physical—is simply a sensation? Suffering doesn't come from pain; it comes from believing that pain shouldn't be happening, and that it is an indication that not only is something wrong with our bodies, but, again, that something needs to be fixed. We turn pain around and make it mean something is wrong, something needs to be fixed, or something should be different. Yet, isn't that what is *causing* the suffering? It's not the physical sensation. Have you ever felt pain and really focused on it? It goes away; it disappears; it moves to another place; it does all kinds of interesting things. It's not the pain that causes the suffering. It's the focus that says, "This shouldn't be happening. Something is wrong with me. I need to be fixed. I'm not okay."

Illness or pain is *not* a sign that something needs to be fixed. Medical doctors will verify that it is the body's way of creating wholeness. Fever, for example, is your body's attempt to regulate its temperature. Even something like vomiting is a way of getting rid of poisons or toxins in our system. The body knows this doesn't belong, so it attempts whatever means necessary to get rid of it. Our bodies are whole. They know how to heal. True, we use doctors and medicine when we need them, but the perfection of our physical state knows how to come to homeostasis. We use doctors and medicine to take away the resistance that we might be feeling so we can remember our wholeness.

Real healing comes when we begin to see the state of wholeness in ourselves or in anyone who we are defining as ill. What are you seeing when you look at someone ill? Are you seeing the illness, or can you look and see wholeness? See beyond the wounds to the perfection. I have taught spiritual practitioners that if they go into a hospital room and see sick people, they should get out immediately; they don't belong there. When you go into the hospital, see the wholeness. Only see the perfection.

Illness of any kind is your body's way of getting your attention about some aspect of your life that is not in balance. One thing you can do to find out what is out of balance and wanting healing is to speak to the parts of your body that aren't functioning well. Ask, "What is your message for me? What's going on? What are you inviting me to know?"

Science and religion both have taught us some important principles:

1. We are born whole.

2. We exist simultaneously on many levels (i.e., body, mind, spirit), which are interconnected and synergistic.

This isn't new. Back in the 1800s, people began realizing that they could be healed through the power of the mind. True health is experienced when all three levels are communicating and in harmony. When we ask, "What is the message in this illness or pain?" usually what we get is an indication that some aspect of our spiritual or mental or physical life just wants more attention. It's not wrong; it does not need to be fixed. It just wants more attention.

Think of the different aspects of your life as spokes on a wheel. If your social life, or sex life, or business life, or creative life is out of whack, the wheel can't ride along smoothly, and something in the body usually gives way. Take a circle and divide it into sections representing different areas or aspects of your life. Then draw a line either close to the center or close to the circumference to represent how complete that area of your life is at this time.

Your creativity might be high, for instance, so you can put a line near the edge. If another area is low, draw the line more toward the center. Do that for every area, and then imagine that wheel trying to turn. What would happen? There would be bumps along the way. These bumps show up in your physical state. The bumps along the way are calling you to focus more on the different aspects of your life.

In our journey to adulthood, we sometimes make choices that gradually reduce our wholeness. These are usually choices that conflict somehow with our core values. Have you ever made a choice and later you found yourself saying, "Where did I go with that one?" These barriers to wholeness reduce our vitality and well-being, as well as our inner guidance. We naturally move back to wholeness as we remove these barriers. Effective care and treatment must focus not only on the outer aspect or the physical, but also on the other two levels of our being. We cannot separate a healthy body from a whole life. Remember the principle that all of life is an inside job. Pain and illness are indicators that some aspect of our life needs more attention. Give it some thought, but be careful not to focus on what's wrong. Remember, what you focus on increases. This is a delicate line to walk. In looking for the message and discerning how to handle physical challenges in your life, be careful to allow yourself to look beyond appearances. Keep your wholeness in mind rather than focusing on what you think needs to be healed.

There is an original blueprint of health embedded in our beings. So in a spiritual sense, there is nothing to heal—only our innate wholeness and perfection that need to be revealed. That's a very different way of looking at life. If you are looking at life from a point of view that you've got to fix it, you've got to heal it, you're constantly broken, what you focus on—brokenness—increases. You get more to fix, more to heal, and more that seems broken. Have you ever noticed that when something breaks around the house, everything else starts to break? Well, it's because you focus on, "Oh, my, this is broken and it needs to be fixed." As you focus on that, broken happens more. Instead, focus on the innate perfection. The deepest healing comes when we truly grasp this truth about ourselves or anyone else whose health and wholeness concerns us.

Ernest Holmes writes in *The Science of Mind*:

> "What the healer does is to mentally uncover and reveal the Truth of Being, which is that God is in and through everyone, and that this Indwelling Presence is already perfect. We separate the belief from the believer and reveal that which needs no healing. Thought is sifted, and that which does not belong to the real

self must be discarded. We really heal the thought. The Spirit of man needs no healing, for the Spirit of man is God."[3]

In the late 1800s, a young woman from a family with a history of consumption (tuberculosis) was desperately ill. She had tried everything medically to cure her consumption, but she was only getting worse. The doctors had written her off completely. At this same time, there was a new movement on the horizon in the United States—one with some radical ideas about healing. It embraced the idea that people could be cured of illness and disease simply through prayer and mental work. This movement was founded on one principle: that we are spiritual beings and we each have a built-in capacity for wholeness. This young woman was convinced by a friend to go hear a lecture. She figured she had nothing to lose, so she convinced her husband to go with her. Her husband didn't think much of the lecture, but she heard one sentence that came as a true revelation to her—her "ah-ha moment." The words she heard and deeply took to heart were: "You are a child of God, and therefore do not inherit illness." She came from a family that all had tuberculosis and the doctors had told her that it was hereditary, it was in her genes.

She left the lecture repeating this statement, and her whole outlook toward herself and her life began to change. Instead of focusing on curing herself from illness, she began to focus on healing—that is, understanding her innate wholeness. She started talking to her body and telling it a new story; and she stuck with this in spite of appearances. Gradually, she began to see herself as whole—which is the real definition of healing—and eventually she was cured. This woman was Myrtle Fillmore, who, along with her husband Charles, eventually became the founder of the Unity Movement and the Unity School of Christianity. The whole basis of Unity is healing prayer and knowing our wholeness.[4]

Dr. Richard Cabot, former dean of Harvard Medical School, supports this belief in the inherent perfection to be revealed. He said:

> "The body simply has a superior wisdom which is biased in favor of life rather than death, and which is ten times as powerful as medicine's initiative. What is this powerful force? It is God, the power upon which all of us depend in order to be here today. I earnestly recommend to the medical profession to let the patient know of this great force that is working within him, working on the patient's side, working on the doctor's side. It does the medical profession no good to avoid the word 'God'; why not teach people the truth?"[5]

Scripture tells us, "Then you will know the truth, and the truth will set you free" (John 8:32). No medicine, no doctor, no focus on disease can make us well. Wholeness is the state of knowing the truth that even our bodies are no less made in the image and likeness of God than our spirit or soul. When we understand this, our next step is to take responsibility and ask for guidance on the cause of the illness.

This step has nothing to do with blame. I'm not suggesting you ask, "What did I do to cause this?" Strike that from your vocabulary. The cause is often so much more complex than some simplistic explanation. Be particularly careful when it comes to trying to figure out the cause for someone else. It's not our business. I used to read earlier books on healing and say to a person, "Oh, you have a cold. It must mean there's some congestion in your thinking!" It scares me to think of the damage I may have done, both to others and myself, by trying to diagnose. Each of us is responsible only for ourselves. Only we can know what needs attention. Remember, it's not about being fixed or finding out what's wrong with us. See any lack of vitality and full health simply as a wake-up call to become more conscious of the connection between your emotions, your living habits, and your body. We are whole beings, and so often we forget that. Remembering that is the greatest gift we can give ourselves during those times when appearances are telling us something else.

We are first and foremost spiritual beings. We are not human beings having a spiritual experience, or even spiritual beings having a human experience. The truth is that we are spiritual beings having a spiritual experience. Sometimes, even "spiritually oriented" people say, "I am not my body." I would caution to be careful of that thinking as well. We are whole; we are spiritmindbody—it's all one word.

That's the truth of who we are. Our bodies are not separate from our minds or our spirit. We see things in physical space and form. There are hundreds of millions of galaxies, but we only see what we can see with our eyes. We think what we see is real and so we think what we see with our physical form is who we are. There is so much more. It's when we begin, even subtly, to forget that truth that we create an imbalance that appears as an illness. Rather than assessing blame, we can look for what will bring the desired movement—the shift—and, eventually, the healing.

We also don't need to feel guilty if we use a doctor, need surgery, or use some form of prescription medicine. While I am a believer in holistic practices, I am aware that when I shun or avoid Western medicine, it's because I am creating separation once again by believing that holistic practices are Go(o)d and other practices are not.

By realizing our wholeness, we can overcome all illness, and perhaps eventually death. I use Jesus as a model; he was able to heal the sick and raise the dead, and he said we can do these things and even greater (John 14:12). I tend to take him at his word. I'm waiting! I recall, however, that we can only manifest at the level of our spiritual understanding.

Since my spiritual understanding is not sufficient to enable me to mentally set bones, or to regrow cartilage that has been depleted, I have had to call in a surgeon. We can go only as far as our spiritual knowledge takes us. Principle is infinite, but we shall demonstrate its power only at the level of our concept of it. If we had the understanding that Jesus had, we would be able to walk on the water. You laugh, but it's the truth. As mentioned in a previous chapter, scientists tell us we use only a small portion of our brains; we know only a small amount of what our real capacity for life is.

If we had the understanding and consciousness that Jesus or Buddha had, we would be able to walk on water. Someday one will come along who knows how to walk on or over water. Be patient with yourself until then. Sometimes the body needs time to catch up with the changes we make in our thoughts and our experience. It's denser. So often when we change our thinking, the body doesn't come along as quickly. It takes a little longer. So many people say, "I've been praying, I've been knowing, but I don't see separation. Why?" Just give it time. Be careful not to abandon the truth and settle back into fear when you are not seeing immediate results. Ernest Holmes said, "If you abandon the truth in your hour of need, it proves that you never did know the truth."[6] Belief beyond appearances is not believing that when things are working, they meet our expectations. It is believing in spite of what we see.

If you were driving from New York to California and got lost for a while in Ohio, you wouldn't say, "Oh, it's no use. I think I'll just turn around and go home because I got lost!" You would keep your focus on where you are heading, rather than turning back or stopping. It's the same with your physical, or spiritual, or emotional ills. Keep your eyes focused on where you are going, and where you are going is where you started. You start in wholeness; you complete in wholeness. When you keep your eyes on that, the stuff along the way just disappears.

It's been said that the *Apollo 11* spacecraft was off course 90 percent of the time during its long voyage to the moon. But the destination was preprogrammed and the spacecraft kept correcting and adjusting its bearings until finally it reached the moon. That is like what we are doing.

Keep your focus on wholeness, and use whatever means necessary to allow your body to experience peace. Gradually try to lead your thoughts from where they might be into the higher realms of consciousness where the soul knows without a doubt that there is no separation from its own I-am-ness.

One of the best questions you can ask is, "How can I bring myself back to what I know to be true—that I am whole, I am safe, I am a perfect manifestation of the divine?" Remember, a higher idea always heals a lesser one. Call in support if need be. That's why, in New Thought Churches, we have licensed and trained ministers, practitioners, and spiritual coaches who can easily know the truth. Use us. (To find a practitioner near you, go to www.religiousscience.org under "Find a Practitioner," or contact me directly at DrToni@tonilamotta.com.) We're really good at seeing the truth for others, and we use each other when we fail to see it for ourselves.

Finally, remember that wholeness doesn't equal perfection, as most people understand it. In the Bible story when the man with the withered hand was made whole, his hand was restored to perfect functionality, but not necessarily perfect appearance (Matt. 12:9–13). In other words, if he had a scar on his pinky, when his withered hand was made whole, the scar was probably still there. I bet if he had a birthmark on his thumb, when his hand was made whole, the birthmark was probably still there.

Wholeness is not about fixing anything. You were never broken! It's not about the perfection that is getting all your expectations met either. It's not about being made perfect—it's about knowing you already are. Claim it and see what happens. You'll experience life differently. I guarantee it.

Chapter 14
Wisdom

"Everything I need is now mine."

One of my favorite writers, Emmet Fox, once said, "God is love, but God is also infinite intelligence, and unless these two qualities are balanced in our lives, we do not get wisdom; for wisdom is the perfect blending of intelligence and love."[1]

Recently someone told me that I portrayed a balance of intelligence and love. That is probably the highest compliment anyone could pay me. The truth is that wisdom is the divine quality that I am most attracted to and prayed for a good deal of my life. I remember as a young child first hearing the Scripture reading from 1 Kings about Solomon praying for wisdom. Then and there, even though I didn't even understand what it meant, I began to do the same. It said that

Solomon prayed for wisdom and all else was given him, so I understood it was the "quick and dirty" way to get wisdom.

I want to share that Scripture with you:

Solomon showed his love for the LORD by walking according to the statutes of his father David, except that he offered sacrifices and burned incense on the high places.

The king went to Gibeon to offer sacrifices, for that was the most important high place, and Solomon offered a thousand burnt offerings on that altar. At Gibeon the LORD appeared to Solomon during the night in a dream, and God said, "Ask for whatever you want me to give you."

Solomon answered, "You have shown great kindness to your servant, my father David, because he was faithful to you and righteous and upright in heart. You have continued this great kindness to him and have given him a son to sit on his throne this very day.

Now, O LORD my God, you have made your servant king in place of my father David. But I am only a little child and do not know how to carry out my duties. Your servant is here among the people you have chosen, a great people, too numerous to count or number. So give your servant a discerning heart to govern your people and to distinguish between right and wrong. For who is able to govern this great people of yours?"

The Lord was pleased that Solomon had asked for this. So God said to him, "Since you have asked for this and not for long life or wealth for yourself, nor have asked for the death of your enemies but for discernment in administering justice, I will do what you have asked. I will give you a wise and discerning heart, so that there will never have been anyone like you, nor will there ever be. Moreover, I will give you what you have not asked for—both riches and honor—so that in your lifetime you will have no equal among kings. And if you walk in my ways and obey my statutes and commands as David your father did, I will give you a long life." (1 Kings 3:3–14)

Have you ever thought to yourself, "What would I do if God came to me with the same offer?" If one day in a dream or an awakened state you heard, "Ask what you wish me to give you"? Would you have the foresight to ask for wisdom? What choice would you make? Our actions often show that we consider many things in our lives as more important, more pressing than wisdom. When was the last time you prayed for wisdom?

A classic joke illustrates this choice in prayer.

An angel appears at a faculty meeting and tells the dean that in return for his unselfish and exemplary behavior, the Lord will reward him with his choice of infinite wealth, wisdom, or beauty. Without hesitating, the dean selects infinite wisdom.

"Done!" says the angel, and disappears in a cloud of smoke and a bolt of lightning.

Now all heads turn toward the dean, who sits surrounded by a faint halo of light. One of his colleagues whispers, "Say something, oh, wise one."

The dean sighs and says, "I should have taken the money."

The truth is that we don't need to ask for wisdom or any of the other qualities, because they are our natural inheritance. The kind of wisdom that I am speaking about is not what comes with age and experience, the wisdom that is a certain way of asking questions, of seeking information, or of looking at the world and making sense of it. That kind of wisdom is important to develop.

However, I am talking about our natural ability to discern that which is right. (Read the chapter on unity to know that I don't believe in right or wrong, but our language doesn't give me any better word to use.) Perhaps a better way to say this is, wisdom is discerning what we truly want, what our higher self knows is in our best interest, or what is most just.

Let me give you another example from the Scripture about Solomon. It's one of the best stories in the Old Testament, and it illustrates in action his wisdom:

A Wise Ruling

Now two prostitutes came to the king and stood before him. One of them said, "My lord, this woman and I live in the same house. I had a baby while she was there with me. The third day after my child was born, this woman also had a baby. We were alone; there was no one in the house but the two of us.

During the night this woman's son died because she lay on him. So she got up in the middle of the night and took my son from my side while I your servant was asleep. She put him by her breast and put her dead son by my breast. The next morning, I got up to nurse my son—and he was dead! But when I looked at him closely in the morning light, I saw that it wasn't the son I had borne."

The other woman said, "No! The living one is my son; the dead one is yours."

But the first one insisted, "No! The dead one is yours; the living one is mine." And so they argued before the king.

The king said, "This one says, 'My son is alive and your son is dead,' while that one says, 'No! Your son is dead and mine is alive.'"

Then the king said, "Bring me a sword." So they brought a sword for the king. He then gave an order: "Cut the living child in two and give half to one and half to the other."

The woman whose son was alive was filled with compassion for her son and said to the king, "Please, my lord, give her the living baby! Don't kill him!" But the other said, "Neither I nor you shall have him. Cut him in two!"

Then the king gave his ruling: "Give the living baby to the first woman. Do not kill him; she is his mother."

When all Israel heard the verdict the king had given, they held the king in awe, because they saw that he had wisdom from God to administer justice. (1 Kings 3:16–28)

We all have within us the ability to discern. We are all born with the gift of wisdom. You know when you know something, even if you choose at the moment to deny it. For example, how many people have taken a job that they knew was not right for them? I can't tell you how many people tell me they knew they were making a mistake in getting married practically from the moment that they walked down the aisle—or at least within the first two weeks. Think of all the times you have said, "I knew that wouldn't work; I just knew I shouldn't have done that." You *knew*; that's the wisdom of God. Let's talk now about how to learn to *listen* to that voice that is always speaking.

Many times when I am counseling people who have come to undo some confusion in their lives, I ask questions to which they always answer, "I don't know." That's what I usually hear.

"What do you really want?"

"I don't know."

"What's troubling you?"

"I don't know."

In my former Neuro-Linguistic Programming (NLP) training, I learned to ask, "What would the answer be *if you did know*?" Invariably, they tell me what they thought they didn't know almost immediately. Wisdom is innate. We know. There's a voice inside each of us that we need to learn to listen to more clearly. We just hide it from ourselves.

Years ago I also studied something called Voice Dialogue, which explains why we sometimes are confused with which voice to listen to. In essence, Voice Dialogue teaches you to talk with and as the different parts of yourself. You personify different parts of yourself and have conversations with yourself. If you *really* listen to people, you can hear when their voices change in conversations. For example, I still sound like a twelve-year-old when I am flirting or when I am nervous. My voice totally changes. Some people's voices get deeper and scolding when they are mimicking a critical parent. Voice Dialogue teaches you to listen to what part of you is speaking at different times in your life.

You also can learn to listen to these voices when they speak inside of you. You don't have to verbalize it, although verbalizing it to someone else is often helpful. When I am talking to someone and I ask, "What are you feeling?" I can often hear the age in his voice. Then it is easy to take him back to see the situation that caused whatever it is that seems to be causing him difficulty now. What we are doing is listening inside of ourselves. We have lots of different voices, and discerning them can be very revealing.

One such voice is the victim. If you listen carefully, you can hear the whining: "It's not my fault. I didn't have anything to do with it." I can hear myself when I go there. Another voice is the critic. Usually this voice is louder than the others and always makes you feel bad: "You shouldn't be doing those things. What's wrong with you? You are never going to amount to anything." Have you ever heard that voice inside of you?

Then there is the voice of the wounded child. In me, it comes out like a two-year-old: "I don't wanna. You can't make me." To this day, I can hear myself go there; and when I can't hear it, I have friends who point it out.

We can do this to support one another. It's actually kind of fun. Simply ask, "How old am I now?" For example, when someone is saying some version of, "I'm not going to do it, I don't wanna, and you can't make me," he usually is frightened or scared; but often it can mean he is angry and afraid to express his anger more fully. Many times it's that wounded child speaking who couldn't say these things when he was little.

Inside of us, we have built-up tension over things we couldn't say. If you want to experience healing over things like this, just go to a safe, comfortable place and begin screaming out the phrases you really want to say. Wonderful healing comes forth. How many ways do we say as an adult, "I'm taking my bat and ball and going home," or, "I'm outta here," or, "I'm through with this." How many times have you said, "I don't want any more of this. I'm done"? What voice is speaking? More than likely, it's the wounded child.

Many times we confuse this voice and we think it's the voice of God. "I'm really disgusted with this job and I've got to get out of here for my own good." Does that sound like God? Does anyone know of a God that speaks like that? It's that child within us.

Then there's the voice of the playful child—there's lots of giggling. I've known clients who can't even talk because they have this nervous laughter going on.

Within all of us there are lots of voices; some people even give them names. I have a friend who can detect the parts of her body that a voice is speaking from. Play with that. Ask yourself when you hear one of these voices, "What part of my body is this voice speaking from right now?" Try it sometime; it's amazing what you'll learn. The way we hear the voice of God is by starting to understand which other voices are out there.

When so many voices are speaking, how do we know which one is spirit? First, spirit's voice is *always* a voice of love. It's never punishment; it's never discipline; and it's never scolding. God only wants our good, and you know when someone really only wants what is your good, because you feel it. Your guts say, "I get that this person is here to support me." You know the difference when someone says, "It's for your own good," when it truly is something that he is saying to support you. That's God speaking.

It could even be correction. We could be asked to change our lives, but the message comes in a gentle touch. It comes in a way that says, "I want more for my life and I don't like the way things are going right now." You might cry and scream and say a few choice words. but all of these moments are gestures of love. You know that is God speaking.

"You had better straighten out; there's something wrong with you" is never the voice of God. *Never.* We are never asked to struggle and we are never punished. Give up the struggle. Source energy does not want struggle or punishment. Have you ever noticed that you never change when someone tells you must change?. However, it's really easy to change when you hear the voice of love instead. We accommodate, we give in, and we change, because we know that that's the voice of love speaking.

If we listen only to our five senses, we get conflicting messages, and we think that what's happening in our lives is inner wisdom—especially when it is negative. Most people say to me, "This is happening. It must be God, or the universe, or the stars, or some form of what's supposed to be happening." What kind of universe sends us all negative circumstances? Remember Einstein's question: is the universe a friendly place? It certainly applies here. When negative circumstances occur, they happen because we don't want to listen to what really is going on; not because God made them happen. I dislike it when insurance companies call tornadoes or horrific accidents "acts of God." We often have the mentality that God speaks through disaster.

Instead, we need to learn to hear the still, small voice. Another Old Testament passage, also from the book of 1 Kings, talks about God not being in wind, earthquake, or fire, but in the still small voice (1 Kings 19:11–12). That's why the practice of daily meditation is so important. It's so important every day to spend time in silence so we can hear the voice of our higher wisdom self and know it from all the other voices. How does that voice sound? How does it feel? Where is it in your body? Do you know? Hearing and recognizing the voice is a practice. I invite you during your meditation to notice how this voice is speaking. For some of us it's in feeling; for some it's in words; for some it's in pictures. We need to notice what the voice of God, our highest wisdom voice, is in our life.

Learning to use the quality of wisdom is all about awakening the power that's already within. It's a most important truth for everyone to learn that source speaks directly *to* us as well as *through* us. The infinite intelligence of the universe is ours if we but learn to listen for it.

I was at a workshop once in which we did an awesome visualization. I invite you to do it now. Imagine a special room that was created to be your office, the most perfect office you could imagine. Sit in that room and notice a computer on your desk that you easily know how to operate. In the computer is the answer to any question you want to know. In fact, you can access any person from the past; you can access any book that has ever been written. The knowledge is already yours. What do you want to know? Who would you like to ask a question?

Actually, this is the kind of access to wisdom that we do have—and that we had long before computers were invented. Within us is the intelligence of the universe. Within us is everything that was ever made or anything that is going to be made. We have this all already within us. God is everywhere present—all of God, not a part of God somewhere. Wherever God is, all of God is present; and if that is true, then all of God is present within you and me, and all of the vast universal intelligence is therefore available to us. That's pretty awesome, don't you think?

So we need to let go of, "I'm confused and I don't know." When we do find ourselves saying that, let us at least acknowledge that we are open to the intelligence of the universe. Recognize that all we need to know is within us. You don't have to go to a seminar. You don't have to go to a sacred place. These are wonderful places, but you don't have to go to Machu Picchu to find wisdom. It's all within you already.

Wise and compassionate guidance is always available in every situation. It is our job to continually assist and support its growth, and to strive to increase awareness of this guidance. It's not about going to get something you don't have; it's about becoming aware of what you already do have. To do this you need to become aware of what you are feeling. If you wish to become aware of your innate wisdom, what universal intelligence is saying, you need to pay attention to your feelings. Following your feelings will lead you to their source. For example, if you hear disturbing news from a friend or read about it in the newspaper, ask yourself, "Why does this news affect me this way? What's going on here for me? Why do I feel so disturbed? Does my experience support my suspicions?"

Have you ever cried at a movie, and then walked away saying that it was a tearjerker? Everyone else in the theater may not be crying even though you are. I sometimes cry at sitcoms. When everyone on or watching TV is laughing, the tears are streaming down my face. In these instances, I want to know what is attempting to speak. There is something I need to hear. Sometimes it happens when I listen to music as well. Something in me got touched deeply. I can ignore it and say, "This is my relaxing time; I'm not going to pay any attention to this," or I can make a mental note and say, "What is this? What am I feeling at this moment, and what does it represent?"

We go through so much of life forgetting to ask this. We need to ask this, not, "What's wrong with me?" We're good at asking that question. If you scold yourself when you cry—"Why am I crying? What's wrong with this? Whose voice is that?"—that's not the voice you want to listen to. Listen for the still, small voice that is calling you to wholeness.

Take note right at the moment when you are feeling emotional. What is the message here? What is that loving voice trying to say? You can cry in the presence of love. Then, you can look and ask what the voice is calling forth. Sometimes I don't get an answer in the moment. But I'll get a flashback or a memory in a dream, or a thought that comes later on, perhaps even in the shower.

We've been told over and over again to "ask and you shall receive"; so when we are in need of wisdom or guidance in a particular decision or life situation, we need to ask, *expecting* the answer to be readily available. Some people forget to ask, and many of us don't really expect to be heard. Wisdom itself speaks through intuition, not through our analytical minds. Trust me. I've spent years figuring that if I just knew enough, I'd get close to God. That's not the way it works. Intuition is a direct communication between the personality and the soul. It's that message that comes through.

A number of speakers I have heard in the past define intuition as "the process of reaching accurate conclusions based on inadequate information." We just *know* something, even though we don't know how we know. The word *intuition* derives from the Latin, *intuere*, meaning "to look within." Intuition is something we see and hear and feel within. It is an internal language that facilitates insight and understanding. This is why I've suggested we get in touch with the inner voices to discern when it is the voice of intuition, rather than all the other voices.

We need to learn to develop some techniques to discipline the mind so as to develop and employ intuition. One technique is to honor emotional cleansing at all times. Keep your emotions current. If you are angry, for example, check that you are really angry about what is happening right now, not about something that happened in the past that is being triggered now. If you are feeling sadness, ask, "Is this sadness related to what's now going on?" If someone just died or you get bad news, you may start to cry; but if you start to cry at a sit-com, it's probably not related to now, but with the past. Do whatever it takes to clear up your emotions.

Spend time each day to clear yourself of emotional impacts. We dispose of physical wastes, so we need to dispose of mental as well. I suggest not going to bed in anger ever. Work with and honor your emotions, and keep them current. Don't put off until tomorrow what you can do today. If you are having an argument with a person, make sure to clear it up. Don't take it to bed. Don't carry it with you in your cells. Don't wait and say, "Someday I'm going to get to clean that up." If something happened today that you don't like, do something about it right now.

We also need a cleansing nutritional program, because physical toxins can interfere with intuition. When we have too much sugar, for instance, we say, "I'm just not thinking straight today." It's almost impossible to hear the voice of God when your body is filled with sugar (dark chocolate excluded!).

We also need to honor the guidance we receive. So often we do hear, but do nothing about it. We say, "I heard the voice; it told me what to do, and I just ignored it." After a while, if you stop listening to and acting on that voice, the voice grows dimmer. If you stop using it, you lose it. You need to be able to listen and act.

Finally, allow yourself an orientation of openness toward your life and the universe. Approach the questions in your life with a sense of faith and trust that there is a reason, a divine purpose, for all that is happening, and that the reason, at its heart, is always compassionate and good. This essential thought needs to be in place in order to activate and cultivate intuition.

You know it is God speaking when it rings true. The only reason you can listen to anything I have to say, for example, is because you already know it. If you are reading this and saying, "Wow, this is great," give yourself credit because of what you are resonating when you hear truth. Anytime you read a book and say, "That was a great book," you are saying, "I already knew that"; because what you are doing is constantly resonating with truth. Truth never contaminates or condemns; it always empowers you. Truth comes to us and we often contaminate it with fear.

We can learn to notice that we are responding to insecurity rather than to truth by asking some questions:

- If I follow what I'm hearing, will it increase my level of enlightenment?

- Will it make me lighter; will it make me freer?

- Will I have more joy, peace, and love?

That's how you can know it's the voice of Wisdom, because that voice always comes with the fruits of the spirit—things like joy, peace, patience, and kindness. All of those things are a result of spirit, so we know it is spirit speaking when that's the effect.

You can always test this. The simplest test of discernment is, "How do my guts feel? Am I at peace with this?" Sometimes we feel fear. In these times, we need to distinguish among the deep feelings. I can feel fear, yet have deep peace at the same time. I can be afraid of moving forward, yet know that it is exactly what I need to do.

Let me make one final point about wisdom and discernment. Sometimes we have to make a very significant decision in our lives. We are pretty sure of it; we feel strongly that we have chosen the perfect response. Still, there is the need for confirmation—not approval—so through our honest communication with at least one other person, we become clearer on our decisions. We are not isolated islands. We were born into community. Scripture says, "For where two or three come together in my name, there am I with them" (Matt. 18:20). Over the years, I have paraphrased it to say, "Where two or three are gathered in my name, there is the I Am presence." It doesn't say when you are sitting alone in your room and you think you know the answers, that is God. I never read that anywhere. Have you? It says, "Where two or three are gathered...." Be open for discernment from those you trust.

Have you noticed that when you think you haven't made up your mind, and someone says he thinks the opposite is true, you get annoyed? You immediately know what you want to do because you have heard the opposite.

It is always a good idea to have your discernment checked. So many factors—some mentioned above—get in the way of our truly distinguishing the voice of God. In graduate school my professor used to call the process of discernment as getting "consensual validation." I used to argue with him that I could make my own decisions and didn't need anyone else; but by the end of the semester, I came to agree with him. I was fighting what I had learned earlier in the convent when we used to talk about Ignatian discernment. This practice included going to the community and finding out if something was valid, if it resonated with more than just me.

When you are going through experiences such as the decision to change a job, a residence, or a significant relationship, even if you are sure of yourself, it's a good idea to verbalize to at least one other person whose wisdom you can trust. I think that's why coaching has become so popular today—not because coaches tell us what to do, but because in their listening we can hear our own truth.

There is so much more power in agreement than in disagreement. If you ever want an intention fulfilled, you can pray for it by yourself; but if you pray for it in a group, the request is given so much more strength and power. I am not saying to abdicate responsibility for your decisions; but know that "where two or three are gathered," there is a special resonance and the I Am presence is more clearly guaranteed.

We are created as unique individuals—in community. Although we are each responsible for our own decisions, we often do not have all the information we need in order to choose well until we enter into real communication with another person. I'm not saying tell everybody. Carefully discern with whom you speak. What seems to affect only us because we are the ones with the particular set of thoughts and feelings actually has ripple effects upon many people. Nothing we do in life affects us alone; it affects everyone around us. Life and spirit are bound together in many more ways than we can recognize at any given moment, especially a moment of personal crisis or decision. Our minds are never as clear at those times.

Listen to the other voices inside you. Start discerning. Have a good friend tell you when your voice changes, and simply laugh and ask yourself, "Who was that speaking? Am I the victim, the wounded child, the critical parent? What's happening right now so I can start to distinguish those voices?"

Wisdom is a divine quality, so it is part of our inherited nature. This is something we've been gifted with. It is not something we have to grasp at. It is not something we have to wait for. It is not something we have to be good enough to get. Wisdom is for all of us. We need to become aware of those still, small voices inside of us. You have heard that voice, or you wouldn't be reading this. That voice brought you here. That voice brings you where there is the presence of God.

I want to end with a prayer familiar to many—"The Serenity Prayer," by Reinhold Niebuhr—but with a slight change:

God, grant me the serenity to

accept the things I cannot change;

the courage to change the things I can;

and *I now accept that I already have the wisdom to know the difference.*[2]

Chapter 15
Uncovering Beliefs

As you begin to focus on your chosen quality, you'll find that amazing things start to happen in your life. Remember, what you focus on increases. When you focus on joy, for example, you'll be looking for things to be joyful about. This is not a onetime, read-the-book and "get it" deal. It's a practice, but it's not a hard practice. In fact, it becomes like a game: How many ways can I see and experience power today? Where is the abundance in this situation, and how am I partaking of it? What makes us one? How are we more alike than different? Could I see this another way so that the beauty shows up? Am I free here, or what would it take to live in the freedom that I know is my heritage?

As I mentioned earlier, sometimes when you first start to focus on something, everything unlike it shows up. Most of us have spent years with unsupportive beliefs and ideas, and sometimes just changing our focus won't change these beliefs as quickly as we'd like. That's when it's time to use an arsenal of spiritual tools to help uncover beliefs that may be hindering us and replace them with beliefs that serve. I have three favorite tools to help do this. I will mention two briefly, and then share one more extensively here.

The first is a technique of prayer based on the beliefs shared in this book, called spiritual mind treatment, or affirmative prayer.

Affirmative Prayer

Most people have learned to pray by begging a God somewhere out there to please change its mind about something and do what they are bidding. The universe operates by law, and the law says, "It is done unto you as you believe." If you believe that this type of prayer works, it does. Most people, however, pray when they don't believe, and then wonder why they get exactly what they were worrying about.

The affirmative prayer is known in some circles as spiritual mind treatment, because it is like a doctor's prescription for our mind. In this form of prayer, we speak from a place of knowing and affirm the truth until we believe it.

Whatever we may be feeling on the surface, deep down, we can still know the truth of our being: that we are made in the image and likeness of God. We can know our true essence; our true self is healthy, whole, and well as we know our oneness with our creator.

When we affirm that we are healthy, abundant, peaceful, or joy-filled, we affirm that we were created to be living fully with all the attributes of our source, our creator.

Affirmative prayer, or spiritual mind treatment, requires us to think and feel in ways that will naturally, lawfully, create what we desire. It's praying as Jesus or Buddha prayed. It's not just wishful thinking or hoping, but it's using the laws of the universe to bring about the experience we desire. "It is done unto you as you believe." Affirmative prayer gives us the opportunity to shift our belief.

You can use the affirmative prayer that follows, or you can go to www.religiousscience.org/wmop_site/forming_prayer.html to learn to write your own.

The universe, all that is, life itself, is one. It is good. I know it as God, source, infinite intelligence, and love. I claim now that that same life is what lives and breathes through me. There is only one life. That life is good, that life is God, that life is my life now. I know that I am one with all the good that exists in this universe. I claim that as the essential nature of my being. I see it. I feel it. I know it now more than ever before. And because I know that this life is a source of (quality of God), I know that this quality is also an expression of my being. Here and now I choose to express this quality into my experience of life in the form of _____ (at this point-claim, see, and feel what your life would be like if this quality were being fully expressed in you)_____. As I accept this good into my life, I give great thanks as I open my heart and mind to receive this good into my experience right here and now. I know that life is "'done unto me as I believe.'" I do believe, and so I release these words into the one mind of God and they return to me fulfilled. And so it is. Amen!

Spiritual Life Coaching

The second tool of choice is using a spiritual life coach. Find a coach who is adept at helping you see your hidden beliefs and who can see and know the truth about who you are, even when you can't. I am currently coaching only a small number of individuals; but I have trained others to do this work and will help to find the right coach for you. If you are interested in finding a coach, just write to me at DrToni@tonilamotta.com.

I use coaches for myself all the time, not for an outside influence on what to think or do, but to get clarity on what I may be thinking unconsciously. I've been privileged to have several awesome coaches who have helped me along my path. One such coach with whom I had the privilege of working for a number of years, Marcia Sutton, used a process with me that I found to be one of the most life-changing practices I've ever experienced. It's called Fear to Faith. Marcia and the *Fear to Faith* cocreator, Lloyd Strom, have given me permission to share this technique with you here. I also encourage you to visit their Web site at www.sacreddays.org to get more insight into this process. Their Web site also contains many other supportive materials.

From Fear to Faith

The opposite of faith is not doubt, but fear. Most of our inactions in life are based on fear, whether conscious or unconscious. Sometimes we can trace specific fears to certain incidents that happened early in life, and it often helps to do that, although it is not always necessary. Most of us have probably picked up some subset of the beliefs that say, "I am not lovable; I am unworthy, unnecessary; I am inadequate or flawed in some way; I am not enough."

Fear is really misplaced faith that there is something opposed to God whose influence and ability may bring us evil. Fear and faith are both fueled by the energy of thought. Rather than fight fear (since what we fight or resists, persists), we need to convert fear into faith. This is done through becoming conscious of what can be seen as "'false beliefs'," or those beliefs that aren't bringing us joy and peace.

The Fear to Faith process is an inner-healing process that uses a prepared worksheet along with a guided meditation. Its purpose is to take you beyond hopes and fears in order to identify the "word of God" (or quality) on which you can build your faith. Additionally, it identifies the "error" in your belief system that will be released through additional spiritual practices (see www.sacreddays.org).

The "Fear to Faith Worksheet" is provided on the next page. Use it to go through the following guided process. (If done in a group, a facilitator can read the following; or, alternatively, you can record it and play it whenever you want to go through this process.)

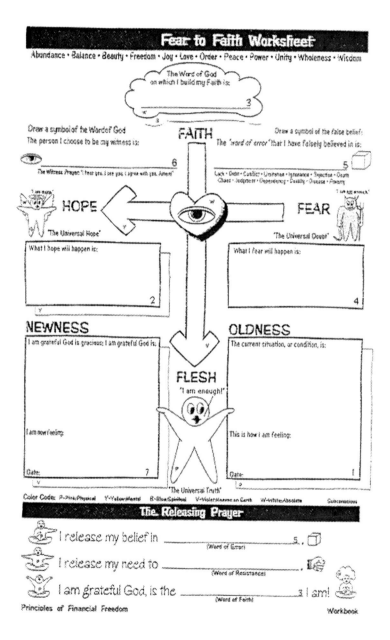

Fear to Faith Worksheet

Abundance • Balance • Beauty • Freedom • Joy • Love • Order • Peace • Power • Unity • Wholeness • Wisdom

The Word of God
on which I build my Faith is:

3

Draw a symbol of the Word of God   **FAITH**   Draw a symbol of the false belief:
The person I choose to be my witness is: The "word of error" that I have falsely believed it is:

6   5

The Witness Prayer: "I hear you, I see you, I agree with you. Amen!"   Lack • Debt • Conflict • Limitation • Ignorance • Rejection • Death
Chaos • Judgment • Dependency • Duality • Disease • Poverty

HOPE   ## FEAR

"The Universal Hope"   "The Universal Doubt"

What I hope will happen is: What I fear will happen is:

2   4

NEWNESS   ## OLDNESS

I am grateful God is gracious; I am grateful God is: The current situation, or condition, is:

I am now feeling: This is how I am feeling:

Date: Date:
7   1

FLESH

"I am enough!"

"The Universal Truth"

Color Code: P=Pink/Physical   Y=Yellow/Mental   B=Blue/Spiritual   V=Violet/Heaven on Earth   W=White/Absolute   Subconscious

The Releasing Prayer

I release my belief in _____ 5.
(Word of Error)

I release my need to _____,
(Word of Resistance)

I am grateful God, is the _____ 3 I am!
(Word of Faith)

Principles of Financial Freedom   Workbook

Find a place where you are comfortable and feeling fully supported by your chair.

(Pause)

Next, bring your awareness to your breathing. Notice as you watch your breath that it becomes deeper and fuller and more balanced.

(Pause)

The breath is the eternal cycle of reception and release within our physical bodies. It is the eternal activity of "God in us."

(Pause)

With every breath you now become more aware and more conscious of the indwelling presence of God, which is your "higher wisdom self."

(Pause)

Now, let your breath serve as a pathway to your heart.

(Pause)

Allow your awareness to move into your heart, for it is here that you begin to see with the "eye of the heart," which is the "eye of wisdom," which is the "eye of love."

(Pause)

Now, in the silence of your heart, ask your "higher wisdom self" to guide you through this process. Ask to have revealed to you every-

thing that you need to know for your highest good and healing …
right here and right now.
(Long Pause)

Step 1. Original Condition

In box number one, in the lower right-hand corner of your worksheet, write a brief description of some troubling condition that you
are currently experiencing that you would like to heal.
(Pause)

Jot down just enough information so that you could look at this
worksheet a month from now and say, "Oh, yeah, I remember that
situation."
(Intuitive Pause)

With one or two words also identify how you feel about this ondition.
(Intuitive Pause)

When you are done, write down today's date in the lower left-hand
corner of box number one.

Step 2. Highest Hope

Now I would like to direct your attention to box number two in the
middle of the worksheet, on the left-hand side under the word

"*Hope.*"
(Pause)

In this box, I invite you to write down what you "hope" will happen as the ultimate outcome of the condition that you described in box number one.
(Writing Pause)

Step 3. Word of God

Now I would like to have you take a moment to close your eyes and go within.
(Long Pause)

Bring your awareness to your breathing and allow yourself to relax completely into the presence of the "divinity that is within you."
(Long Pause)

As you enter into an expanded awareness of your inner self, use the power of your mind to imagine that what you "hope will happen" has already happened.
(Long Pause)

Notice where you are ... who you are with ... what you are doing....
Notice how you are feeling about the situation.
(Intuitive Pause)

Now, let your higher wisdom self magnify the feelings of this experience so that it becomes completely real for you.

(Long Pause)

In the felt reality of this experience, see if you can identify the one quality of God that seems to be most in expression.

(Pause)

It might be love, or peace, or wisdom, or beauty, or joy, or wholeness.

(Pause)

Simply identify that one single word of God that seems to best describe the quality of the situation that you have imagined.

(Pause)

If you are having difficulty identifying this word, ask your higher wisdom self to reveal it to you. Or you may wish to open your eyes and refer to the God qualities listed across the top of the sheet.

(Intuitive Pause)

Once you know what your word is, open your eyes and write it down on line number three in the little cloud at the top of the worksheet.

(Writing Pause)

Working with Icons (Optional):

As a way to invite your "whole brain" into this process, draw a simple little symbol, image, or icon that best represents your "word of faith" in the space provided in the upper left-hand corner of your work-sheet, just to the left of the "cloud." When you are finished, circle this icon to indicate that you are accepting it.

(Writing Pause)

Step 4. Hidden Fear

Now we come to the challenging part of this process. We must face our fears simply so we can explain why they are not so.

(Pause)

We are going to use the energy of our word of God to provide the light that will dispel the darkness of our hidden fears.

(Pause)

Go now to box number four, in the middle of the worksheet, on the right-hand side under the word *"Fear."*

(Pause)

Take a moment to look within and see if you can connect with the fear that you have about the condition that you described in box number one, at the beginning of this process.

(Long Pause)

See if you can identify what it is that you fear might happen as the ultimate outcome of the situation. One common fear is that condition or situation will never change. Another one is that it will become even worse.

(Intuitive Pause)

Write down what you fear might happen in box number four.

(Writing Pause)

Step 5. Word of Error

Now I would like to have you take a moment to close your eyes and go within.

(Long Pause)

Bring your awareness to your breathing and allow yourself to relax completely into the presence of the "divinity that is within you."

(Long Pause)

As you enter into an expanded awareness of your inner self, use the power of your mind to imagine that what you "fear might happen" is happening in your awareness right now.

(Pause)

Remember that your feelings can't hurt you and that God is with you, now!

(Long Pause)

Notice where you are ... who you are with ... what you are doing....
Notice how you are feeling.
(Intuitive Pause)

Now, let your higher wisdom self magnify the feelings of this experience so that they become completely real for you.
(Long Pause)

In the felt reality of this experience, see if you can identify the one single "word of error" that best describes the fear that you are feeling.
(Pause)

It might be a word like *poverty*, or *disease*, or *rejection*, or maybe even *death*.
(Pause)

Simply identify this one single word that when you hear it, it brings up the feelings that you are feeling right now.
(Pause)

If you are having difficulty identifying this word, ask your higher wisdom self to reveal the word to you.
(Intuitive Pause)

Once you know what your "word of error" is, open your eyes and write it down on line number five, next to the little gray "mental block" icon.

(Writing Pause)

Working with Icons (Optional):

As a way to invite your "whole brain" into this process, draw a simple little symbol, image, or icon that best represents your "word of error" in the little gray "circle and slash" in the upper right corner of your worksheet. After you have drawn your "word of error" icon, trace over the gray "circle and slash" to indicate that you are releasing this belief from your consciousness.

(Writing Pause)

Step 6. Word of Resistance

Now take a moment and go within and remember the last time that you experienced fear about the "word of error" that you have just identified.

(Pause)

Allow your higher wisdom self to draw into your awareness an image that best represents what you normally do in reaction to experiencing your "word of error."

(Pause)

Simply notice where you are and what you are doing.
(Intuitive Pause)

Now ask your higher wisdom self to provide you with a single word that best captures the essence of what you usually do to keep your "word of error" from happening.
(Pause)

It may be an outer behavior such as "control." Or it may be an inner activity such as "worry." Simply allow your higher wisdom self to reveal this word to you.
(Intuitive Pause)

Once you know what your "word of resistance" is, open your eyes and write it down on line number six, next to the little "clenched fist" Icon.
(Writing Pause)

Step 7. Newness

Newness begins with the releasing of what is "old" and no longer serves us. There is no more powerful way to release what is old and bring in what is new than to confess our "errors" and affirm our aspirations to another human being. This is simple act "humbles" us and "opens" us up to the grace of God.
(Pause)

Close your eyes and go within once again.

(Pause)

Bring your awareness to your breathing and allow yourself to relax completely into the presence of the "divinity that is within you."

(Long Pause)

Allow your higher wisdom self to draw into your awareness an image or felt presence of someone in your life with whom you would be willing to share the contents of this worksheet.

(Pause)

It might be your prayer partner, a family member or friend.

(Pause)

There is nothing that this person needs to do except to listen to your confession of error and to agree with your intention for a greater expression of your life.

(Intuitive Pause)

Once you know who this individual is, open your eyes and write his or her name next to the little "mind's eye" icon in the upper portion of box number seven in the lower left-hand side of the worksheet.

(Writing Pause)

The final step of the process cannot be completed at this time. We do not yet know what the final outcome will be. It may look like what we "hope will happen." Or it may be an even better outcome that we cannot even conceive of at this time. Box number seven in the lower left corner of the worksheet must be filled out in the future, once the original troubling condition has been resolved.

Step 8. Releasing Prayer

Go to the "Releasing Prayer" section at the bottom of the worksheet. (Pause)

In the blank space of the first line, write in the "word of error" that you previously identified on line number five next to the little "mental lock" icon.
(Writing Pause)

In the blank space of the second or middle line, write the "word of resistance" that you previously identified on line number six next to the little "clenched fist" icon.
(Writing Pause)

In the blank space of the bottom line, write in the "word of faith" that you previously identified on line number three in the cloud at the top of the page.
(Writing Pause)

End of Meditation

The second process, What Happened Wisdom Tree, is an inner-healing process that uses a prepared worksheet facilitated by a guided meditation. Its purpose is to take you back to a remembrance of the originating condition that created your "error belief." Additionally, it identifies a greater spiritual truth that will release and replace the errors in your thinking born out of a misunderstanding of past experiences.

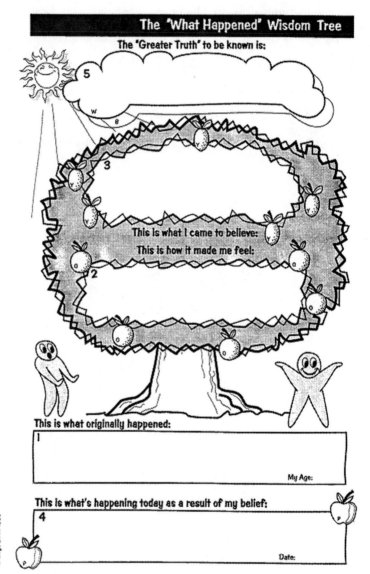

Find a place where you are comfortable and feeling fully supported by your chair.

(Pause)

Next, bring your awareness to your breathing. Notice as you watch your breath that it becomes deeper and fuller and more balanced.

(Pause)

The breath is the eternal cycle of reception and release within our physical bodies. It is the eternal activity of "God in us."

(Pause)

With every breath you now become more aware and more conscious of the indwelling presence of God, which is your "higher wisdom self."

(Pause)

Now, let your breath serve as a pathway to your heart.

(Pause)

Allow your awareness to move into your heart. For it is here that you begin to see with the "eye of the heart," which is the "eye of wisdom," which is the "eye of Love."

(Pause)

And now, in the silence of your heart, ask your "higher wisdom self" to guide you through this process. Ask to have revealed to you everything that you need to know for your highest good and healing, right here and right now.

(Long Pause)

1. Going Back

Now, ask your higher wisdom self to scroll back into time and to draw up into your awareness one of your very first or most formative experiences with your "word of error."

(Pause)

Allow your higher wisdom self to draw into your awareness a significant experience with your word of error" that occurred early in your life.

(Pause)

It could be either a positive or negative experience. Either way, it created deeply held beliefs in you that are operating in your life today.

(Long Pause)

Now, look around you and notice what's happening. Notice where you are ... who you are with ... what you are doing ... how you are feeling ... and perhaps how old you are.

(Intuitive Pause)

Now, let your higher wisdom self magnify the feelings of this experience, so that they become completely real for you.

(Long Pause)

Now, ask your higher wisdom self to show you what you came to believe about your "word of error" as the result of what you felt in this experience.

(Intuitive Pause)

2. The Greater Truth

Now, ask your higher wisdom self to bring you forward into the present time and show you how these deeply held beliefs are being expressed in your life today.

(Pause)

Observe what is happening in your current life experience that expresses the beliefs that were created so very long ago.

(Pause)

Can you see the same feelings and emotional reactions being played out in your life again today?

(Intuitive Pause)

Now, in this present moment, allow your higher wisdom self to reveal to you some greater truth that will set you free from the limiting

beliefs that you have held from the past.
(Pause)

What is the greater truth that will set you free this day?
(Intuitive Pause)

Have your higher wisdom self show you some place in your life today where this greater truth is already being expressed.
(Intuitive Pause)

3. Giving Thanks

Now, thank your "higher wisdom self" for the guidance, direction, and protection that has been given throughout this entire process.
(Pause)

Most especially, give thanks for the wisdom and the understanding that has been revealed to you.
(Pause)

Now, bring your awareness back to your breathing. Feel the movement of the breath in your body.
(Pause)

Feel the presence of your body in the room. Feel your feet on the floor and your body in your chair.
(Pause)

And now, when you're ready, open your eyes and allow your awareness to come gently back into the room.

(Long Pause)

End of Meditation

At this point, you may want to create an affirmative prayer to support you in releasing the belief that you found. You might also find that during the days that follow this exercise, you become increasingly aware of how all-pervasive that belief has been and where it has hindered you in your life. Rejoice! This is a sign that you are truly ready to release this belief and that incredible freedom is about to be uncovered. Use these processes over and over as needed and remember to stay focused on the good that is being revealed.

Enjoy the process, and let me hear your results. Write to me at DrToni@tonilamotta.com. With your permission, you may see your story in a follow-up book!

Endnotes

All Scripture references unless otherwise noted are from the New International Version (NIV) Copyright © 1973, 1978, 1984 by International Bible Society.

Introduction

1. Underhill, Evelyn, *Mysticism: The Nature and Development of Spiritual Consciousness,* (Oxford, England: Oneworld, 1993).

Chapter I

1. Keepin, Will, *Lifework of David Bohm-River of Truth* http://www.vision.net.au/~apaterson/science/david_bohm.htm
2. Holmes, Ernest, *The Science of Mind,* (New York: 1st Jeremy P. Tarcher/Putnam Ed edition, 1997).
3. Fox, Emmet, *The Golden Key*, (Florida: SPS Publications, 2005).

Chapter II

1. Lao Tzu, Stephen Mitchell (Translator), *Tao Te Ching: A New English Version,* (New York: Harper Collins Perennial Classics, 1988).

Chapter III

1. Toothless Grin—Foundation for a Better life http://www.fora betterlife.org.

2. Walsch, Neale Donald, *Communion with God: An Uncommon Dialogue*, (Hardcover) (New York: Putnam Adult, 2000).

3. Abraham-Hicks, Excerpted from the workshop in San Antonio, TX on Saturday, May 17th, 1997.

4. Dyer, Wayne, *The Power of Intention*, (California: Hay House, 2005).

5. Dalai Lama, *Art of Happiness*, (United Kingdom: New English Library, 1999).

6. Holmes, op.cit.

Chapter IV

1. Yogananda, Paramahansa, *Inner Peace: How To Be Calmly Active and Actively Calm,* (California: Self-Realization Fellowship Publishers, 1999).

2. Covey, Stephen R., *The 7 Habits of Highly Effective People*, (New York: Free Press, 2004).

3. Carroll, Lewis and Martin Gardner, *Alice's Adventures in Wonderland and Through the Looking Glass,* (New York: Signet Classics Mass Market Paperback, 2000).

Chapter V

1 Gibran, Kahlil, *The Prophet*, (New York: Alfred A. Knopf; 47th edition, 1923).

2. Browning, Robert, Tyas Harden, Percy Bysshe Shelley, Harry Buxton Forman, and William Groser, *The Works of Percy Bysshe Shelley in Verse and Prose*, (California: Reeves and Turner, 1880). Digitized Jul 13, 2007.

3. Coleman, Earle Jerome, *Creativity and Spirituality: Bonds Between Art and Religion*, (Albany, NY: State University of New York Press, 1998).

4. Emerson, Ralph Waldo, *Art, from Essays: First Series*, (New York: David McKay Company, Incorporated, 1888).

5. Albert Einstein (from http://www.Futurehealth.org).

6. Cornell, Joseph, *With Beauty Before Me*, (California: Dawn Publications, 2000).

7. http://www.sfheart.com/beauty_quotes.html.

8. Costello-Forshey, Cheryl, *The Most Beautiful Flower*—reprinted with permission.

Chapter VI

1. Hubbard, Barbara Marx, *Conscious Evolution: Awakening the Power of Our Social Potential*, (New York: New World Library, 1998).

2. Columbus, Chris, (Director), *Harry Potter and the Chamber of Secrets* (Full Screen Edition) (Harry Potter 2) DVD, April 11, 2003).

3. Williamson, Marianne, *A Return to Love: Reflections on the Principles of a Course in Miracles,* (New York: HarperCollins, 1996).

4. Holmes, Ernest, op. cit.

Chapter VII

1. Chardin, Pierre Teilhard, *The Divine Milieu*, (New York: Harper Perennial Modern Classics; 1st edition, 1960).

2. Maharaj, Nisargadatta, and Jean Dunn, *Consciousness and the Absolute: The Final Talks of Sri Nisargadatta Maharaj,* (New York: Acorn Press, 1994).

3. Foundation for Inner Peace, *A Course in Miracles: Combined Volume* (Hardcover) (New York: Viking Adult; 2nd edition, 1996).

4. Holmes, Ernest, *op.cit.*

5. *Christopher News Note*s, August, 1993.

Chapter VIII

1. Covey, Steven, op. cit.

2. Hugo, Victor, *Les Miserables,* (New York: Fawcett; Mass Market Paperback, 1982).

3. Course in Miracles, op. cit.

4. Chardin, Pierre Teilhard, op. cit.

5. Author unknown first quoted in *The Little Brown Book of Anecodotes.*

6. Fromm, Eric, *The Art of Loving*, (New York: Perennial, 1989).

7. Roosevelt, Eleanor, *This Is My Story, 1937,* http://en.wikiquote.org/wiki/Eleanor_Roosevelt

Chapter X

1 Hanh, Thich Nhat, *Creating True Peace*, (New York: Free Press, 2003).

2. Goldsmith, Joel, http://www.joelgoldsmith.com

3. Goldsmith, Joel, *The Infinite Way*, (California: DeVorss & Company, New Ed edition, 1979).

4. Ibid.

5. Hanh, Thich Nhat, *The Heart of the Buddha's Teaching,* (Paperback), (New York: Broadway, New Ed edition, 1999).

6. Hanh, Thich Nhat, *Creating True Peace.* Op. cit.

Chapter XI

1, Hawkins, David, *Power vs. Force: The Hidden Determinants of Human Behavior*, (California: Hay House, 2002).

2. *Creative Thought Magazine*, http://www.rsintl.org/ctmagazine/default.asp.

Chapter XIII

1. Canfield, Jack, Mark Victor Hansen, Maida Rogerson, Martin Rutte and Tim Clauss, Extracted from Chicken Soup for the Soul: Home Delivery, "How Much is Enough?" from *Chicken Soup for the Soul at Work*, (Florida: HCI, 1996).

2. Waterhouse, Dr. John, *Five Steps to Freedom*, (Florida: Rampart Press, 2003).

3. Holmes, Ernest, op.cit.

4. Witherspoon, Thomas E., *Myrtle Fillmore, Mother of Unity*, (Kansas City: Unity Books (Unity School of Christianity), 3rd edition, 2000).

5. Cabot, Richard C. and Russell L. Dicks, *The Art Of Ministering To The Sick*, (New York: The Macmillan Company, 1936).

6. Holmes, Ernest, op.cit.

Chapter XIV

1. Fox, Emmet, *Around the Year with Emmet Fox: A Book of Daily Readings*, (New York: HarperOne; 2 edition, 1992).

2. Sifton, Elisabeth, *The Serenity Prayer: Faith and Politics in Times of Peace and War*, (New York: W. W. Norton & Company, 2003).

Chapter XV

1. Strom, Lloyd and Marcia Sutton, *Fear to Faith*, http://www. sacreddays.org.

Selected Bibliography

Cabot, Richard, and Russell L. Dicks, *The Art Of Ministering to the Sick*, New York: The Macmillan Company, 1936.

Carroll, Lewis and Gardner, Martin, *Alice's Adventures in Wonderland and Through the Looking Glass,* New York: Signet Classics Mass Market Paperback, 2000.

Chardin, Pierre Teilhard, *The Divine Milieu*, New York: Harper Perennial Modern Classics; 1 edition, 1960.

Covey, Stephen R., *The 7 Habits of Highly Effective People,* New York: Free Press, 2004.

Dalai Lama, *Art of Happiness*, United Kingdom: New English Library, 1999.

Dyer, Wayne, *The Power of Intention*, California: Hay House, 2005.

Emerson, Ralph Waldo, *Art, from Essays: First Series*. New York: David McKay Company, Incorporated, 1888.

Foundation for Inner Peace, *A Course in Miracles: Combined Volume* (Hardcover), New York: Viking Adult; 2 edition, 1996.

Fox, Emmet, *Around the Year with Emmet Fox: A Book of Daily Readings,* New York: Harper One; 2 edition, 1992.

Fox, Emmet, *The Golden Key,* Florida: SPS Publications, 2005.

Fromm, Eric, *The Art of Loving,* New York: Perennial, 1989.

Gibran, Kahlil, *The Prophet,* New York: Alfred A. Knopf; 47th edition, 1923.

Goldsmith, Joel, *The Infinite Way,* California: DeVorss & Company, New Ed edition, 1979.

Goldsmith, Joel, *Practicing the Presence,* California: Harper San Francisco, 1958.

Hanh, Thich Nhat, *Creating True Peace,* New York: Free Press, 2003.

Hanh, Thich Nhat, *The Heart of the Buddha's Teaching* (Paperback), New York: Broadway, New Ed edition, 1999.

Hawkins, David, *Power vs. Force: The Hidden Determinants of Human Behavior,* California: Hay House, 2002.

Hicks, Esther and Jerry, *The Law of Attraction,* California: Hay House, 2006.

Holmes, Ernest, *Creative Mind*, New Mexico: Sun Publishing Company, 1919.

Holmes, Ernest, *The Science of Mind*, New York: 1st Jeremy P. Tarcher/Putnam Ed edition, 1997.

Hubbard, Barbara Marx, *Conscious Evolution: Awakening the Power of Our Social Potential*, New York: New World Library, 1998.

Lao Tzu , Stephen Mitchell (Translator), *Tao Te Ching: A New English Version*, New York: Harper Collins Perennial Classics, 1988.

Progoff, Ira, *At a Journal Workshop: Writing to Access the Power of the Unconscious and Evoke Creative Ability*, California: Tarcher; Revised edition, 1992.

Roth, Ron, *Prayer and the Five Stages of Healing*, California, Hay House, 1999.

Sifton, Elisabeth, *The Serenity Prayer: Faith and Politics in Times of Peace and War,* New York: W. W. Norton & Company, 2003.

Underhill, Evelyn, *Mysticism: The Nature and Development of Spiritual Consciousness,* Oxford, England: Oneworld, 1993.

Vitale, Joe and Ihaleakala Hew Len, *Zero Limits*, New York: John Wiley & Sons, 2007.

Walsch, Neale Donald, *Communion with God: An Uncommon Dialogue,* (Hardcover), Putnam Adult, 2000.

Waterhouse, Dr. John, *Five Steps to Freedom*, Florida: Rampart Press, 2003.

Williamson, Marianne, *A Return to Love: Reflections on the Principles of a Course in Miracles,* New York: HarperCollins, 1996.

Witherspoon, Thomas E., *Myrtle Fillmore, Mother of Unity*, Kansas City: Unity Books (Unity School of Christianity), 3 edition, 2000.

Yogananda, Paramahansa, *Inner Peace: How To Be Calmly Active and Actively Calm,* California: Self-Realization Fellowship Publishers, 1999.

About the Author

Dr. Toni LaMotta, is a provocative and inspiring speaker, writer, and highly regarded spiritual coach. She is an expert in facilitating personal and organizational change. She is currently the Director of In-Lightened Enterprises, LLC, an Internet-based organization which supports women reinventing themselves from the inside out. She was the Founding and Senior Minister of the Sarasota Celebration Center. She is also the author of *Recognition: The Quality Way*.

Dr. Toni specializes in supporting women who are reinventing themselves from the inside out. She's been through a number of reinventions herself, and her broad range of experiences have brought her in front of audiences at some of the top U.S. companies including IBM, AT&T, and Pennzoil as well as college and high students. She served as a Catholic nun and pastoral associate for sixteen years before discovering New Thought and becoming a minister twelve years ago.

She holds a doctorate in religious studies as well as a doctor of divinity degree; three master's degrees—in pastoral ministry, adult education, and mathematics. She also spent ten years as an adjunct faculty member for Baker Online in Michigan, and the University of

Phoenix School of Management & Business both in San Diego and UOP Online.

As a speaker and presenter, Toni is challenging and provocative as she shares insights gained through years of experiences on a spiritual path. Her wit and wisdom speak to both the head and the heart. Her fascinating life journey has led to a depth of compassion, personal growth, and understanding that is truly inspiring. She recently went to the Golden City in Chennai, India where she attended a twenty-one-day process and was initiated as a Oneness Facilitator with the ability to transfer Amma Bhagavan's Oneness Blessing.

Dr. Toni currently lives in Sarasota, Floridal, surrounded by beauty, order, and a great deal of love.

For More Information

For a copy of Dr. Toni's newsletter and free CD, or to hire Dr. Toni as an inspirational keynote speaker for your association or group, contact her through www.tonilamotta.com.

To make comments on Dr. Toni's blog, go to <u>www.Inlightened Enterprises.com</u> Be sure to subscribe to Dr. Toni's weekly newsletter, www.ReinventMidlife.com.

For those who like to *listen* as well as read, Dr. Toni offers two other options:

1. You can receive monthly MP3s of each of the qualities. Go to www.ReinventMidlife.com/audiofocus.htm.

2. You can buy the full set of CDs. You will receive a substantial discount because you have purchased this book. Go to www.ReinventMidlife.com/ddbookoffer.htm.

978-0-595-45429-7
0-595-45429-1